Travelling Through The Promised Land

Donald Bridge

CFP

© Donald Bridge
ISBN 1 85792 272 7
Published in 1998
by
Christian Focus Publications, Geanies House, Fearn, Ross-shire,
IV20 1TW, Great Britain
Cover design by Donna Macleod

Maps by Holmwood, Kirkhill, Inverness, IV5 7QB

Contents

Maps

Introduction

An English Christian leader in Jerusalem (now retired) some-times took shelter in a sardonic sense of humour. His re-marks included, 'No-one who works in this city can be alto-gether normal', 'If any-one tells you that God has sent him to Jerusalem, run for cover', and 'It's amazing how many peo-ple can write a balanced and comprehensive book on Israel, after one eight-day visit!'

Perhaps the first two comments can be applied to me. But as for the third, this book can claim rather more authority than a few reflections gathered from a quick package-tour. As well as organising and leading many Holy Land pilgrim-age-holidays, I have engaged in two preaching and fact-find-ing journeys in that fascinating and lovely land. I spent the summer of 1981 on a sabbatical course at the Hebrew Uni-versity on Mount Scopus, a half-hour walk from the Old City. In 1984 and 1985 I spent the most exciting and colourful fourteen months of my life, resident in East Jerusalem as chaplain of the Garden Tomb. Since then, I have paid a fur-ther study visit, and conducted several more Christian tours.

I returned to Britain in 1985, armed with bulging note-book and diaries, a thousand 2x2 slides, three hundred pho-tographic prints, and dozens of invitations to lecture, teach or preach in the UK and the USA on subjects related to the Land and the Book. Fulfilling these engagements led me into some hair-raising adventures. During those travels I wrote three books, the second of which was *Living In The Prom-ised Land* (Kingsway, 1989, translated into German as 'Kein Land Wie Dieses', Dynamis Verlag, 1990). This offered a kind of literary ramble through the areas where most of the biblical events happened, commenting along the way, on matters geographical, historical and biblical. This current volume represents a comprehensive re-writing and re-structuring of that book, with a subtle but important difference in purpose. I now invite the reader to explore the land with me, as we follow biblical events *in their scriptural and chronological order*. So, for example, we walk with Abraham in chapter 2, David to Jeremiah in chapter 6, the Galilee disciples in chapter 7, and the Early Church in chapter 13.

Although the opening chapter remains very much the same, the rest is so amended and supplemented that what I now offer is a new book, not just a fresh title. In particular, the chapters called, 'Prophets, priests and poets', 'For Zion's sake', and 'Build my church', are entirely new. Eagle-eyed readers of both versions (if such there be) will observe that I have also added recent archaeological discoveries and insights to almost every other chapter, and have in some cases had to revise some of my more tentative opinions (one example is the authenticity of some parts of the Via Dolorosa).

I have removed altogether the closing chapter of the 1989 book, which was called 'Prophecy, Politics and the People of God'. This does not imply that I regret what I wrote then (I don't), but I feel on reflection that such a vast and sensitive topic (the current situation in the Middle East and its relation to the purposes of God) is far too complex to examine in one short chapter.

I am immensely grateful to those who have assisted me with information, ideas, help in travelling, and access to sites. I want to thank in particular Frinton Free Church and the Baptist Union of Great Britain for having made my 1981 sabbatical possible, and to the British Friends of the Hebrew University and the administrators of the University itself for making it so informative. I am deeply grateful to the Committee of the Garden Tomb Association for entrusting to me for fourteen months a chaplaincy that normally lasts two to three months. On several occasions Maranatha Tours (Euro) Ltd have helped me with their considerable professional skills. Kingsway Publications kindly released back to me the copyright of the original 'Living In The Promised Land'. Christian Focus Publications have cordially co-operated in every way with my efforts to make this second volume a record worthy of the fascinating subject it addresses.

Those outstanding scholars Jim Fleming and Kenneth Bailey are not likely to remember their conversations with me, but the grateful memory is still vivid to me. That affable academic, Professor Dan Bahat has enlightened me more than once: I thank him and wish him well in his present work as Chief Archaeologist for the City of Jerusalem.

Most of all, my warmest thanks are due to my dear wife Rita. She rarely appears on the printed page, yet she was my companion in most of the adventures and discoveries related. Her wish, in this and every other part of my life's ministry, has been to take a quiet supporting role. But without her, there would be little ministry worth recording. To her I dedicate this book, with affection and gratitude.

A word of explanation

In any living and developing situation, words and names have the disconcerting habit of changing their meaning. I want to explain and defend my use of phrases like Israel, Palestine, Holy Land and Promised Land in this book. I have a reason for this. I notice an increasing and unfortunate tendency amongst Christians to take up extreme positions on matters

where equally devout Bible-believers may well differ, and
then imagine sinister double-meanings in each others' use of
certain words. So, for example, a reference to the Holy Land
is seen as reluctance to acknowledge the right of Israel to
statehood. Conversely, any use of the word Israel is regarded
by some as a statement of a particular prophetic stance, an
attack on Arabic Christians, or a denial of any Palestinian
right to an opinion.

We can all get confused by these terms, especially as their
usage changes over the years. The first time a Christian introduced himself to me as a Palestinian, I took a half step
backward, wondering nervously where he kept his bombs
and guns, for to me the word meant 'terrorist'! In fact his use
of the term had no political or religious undertones; my correct response should have been, 'Pleased to meet you, I'm
an Englishman.'

So, let me explain my use of words like Israel, Israeli,
Palestine, Palestinian, Holy Land and Promised Land. Readers who have no problems with this (a majority, I suspect)
might be well advised to skip the next two pages, and get
into the real book. People with a nervous disposition might
like to follow suit.

The area promised to Abraham and his offspring was at
that time called Canaan (Gen. 12:1-9). After Jacob's
descendants (the children of Israel) occupied it under the
leadership of Joshua, it was sometimes called Israel, although
that name more often referred to the *people* in covenant with
God (Judg. 21:25). After the great reigns of David and
Solomon, the tribes split into two rival kingdoms, with the
rebel majority in the north keeping the name Israel, whilst
the southern minority, faithful to David's line, took the name
Judah, after its principal tribe (1 Kgs. 12:16-17). To add to

the modern reader's confusion, the *land* of the northern kingdom soon came to be called Samaria, after its capital city (1 Kgs. 18:1-2).

When the northern kingdom went into exile (the so-called lost ten tribes of Israel) the land was re-populated with mixed races who became known as Samaritans (2 Kgs. 17:21-40). The southern kingdom later went into exile too, but some of the captives were later allowed to return (Ezra and Nehemiah). Judah now became Judea, a region or province subject to successive Persian, Greek and Roman overlords.

By the time of our Lord Jesus Christ, Judea was an administrative area within the Roman province of Syria (Matt. 2:1). The Jewish *people*, whether in Judea or in the worldwide 'diaspora', were corporately described as 'Israel', or 'the Jews' (Acts 2:36 and Rom. 1:16).

After 150 AD, the Romans re-named the whole area as Palestina, or Palestine, a name that was to stick for eighteen centuries. Most Jews were expelled, but always some remained in the land. Christendom increasingly referred to the area as the Holy Land, for obvious reasons. The Crusaders, during one of Christianity's most discreditable episodes, often spoke of 'the holy land and the holy places'. Christians and Jews also spoke of 'the Promised Land', again for obvious reasons. Christians sometimes spiritualised that term, to mean either the life of faith or life in 'heaven'.

The land was still called Palestine in 1917, when the British wrested it from Turkish control and began to 'administer' it on behalf of the League of Nations and the United Nations. Odd though it seems now, people born in the land, whether Jewish, Arab or Turkish, often referred to themselves as Palestinians.

With the immigration to Palestine of huge numbers of Jews

from Europe, and the establishment of a sovereign Jewish
state, the name 'Israel' was chosen out of several alterna-
tives, and the new term 'Israelis' was coined for its citizens.
The great majority of these were Jews, but several thousand
Arab Christians (especially in Nazareth) and many Druze
(in the Carmel area) also became citizens of Israel.

'Palestinian' now became the most common descriptive
name for Arabic residents in (and refugees from) the land
west of the river Jordan, all of which was occupied by Israel
in 1967. In accordance with the current 'peace plan', many
of these areas at present remain under Israeli rule, but with
local affairs conducted by semi-autonomous 'Palestinian
authorities'. The best known examples are Gaza, Bethlehem,
Jericho and Nablus (ancient Samaria).

Accordingly, in this book, I refer to the *state* as Israel, the
land as either Israel, Promised Land or Holy Land, its *citizens* as Israelis, and the *Arabic populace* as either Arabs or
Palestinians. No sinister double meanings are intended, and
none should be deduced.

Part One

The Land

What is needed by the reader of the Bible is some idea of the main outlines of Palestine – its shape and disposition; its plains, passes and mountains; its rains, winds and temperatures; its colours, lights and shades. Students of the Bible desire to see a background and to feel an atmosphere (George Adam Smith).

> The LORD your God is bringing you into a good land -
> a land with streams and pools of water,
> with springs flowing in the valleys and hills,
> a land with wheat and barley,
> vines and fig-trees, pomegranates, olive oil and honey,
> a land where bread will not be scarce
> and you will lack nothing.
> (Deuteronomy 8:7-9)

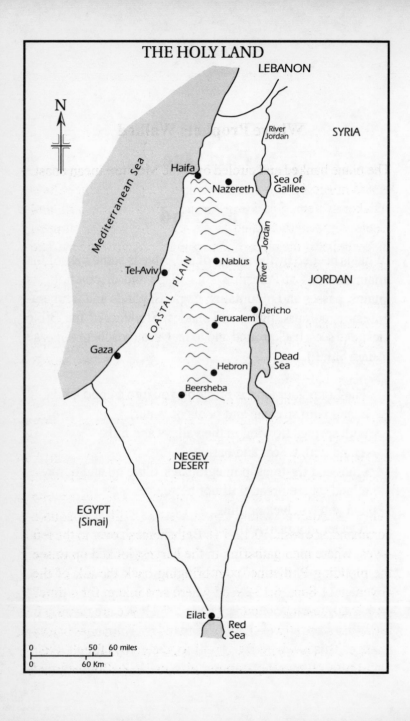

THE HOLY LAND

LEBANON

N

SYRIA

River
Jordan

Mediterranean Sea

Haifa

Nazereth

Sea of
Galilee

River Jordan

COASTAL PLAIN

Tel-Aviv

Nablus

JORDAN

Jerusalem

Jericho

Gaza

Hebron

Dead
Sea

Beersheba

NEGEV
DESERT

EGYPT
(Sinai)

Eilat

Red
Sea

0   50   60 miles
0   60 Km

1

Where Prophets Walked

The plane banked and circled over the Mediterranean coast. Israeli music, joyous and spirited, echoed across the pilot's speaker-system. Sparkling turquoise sea, white hills and luscious greenery floated into view. The wheels bumped twice and now the plane was taxi-ing along the runway. The passengers applauded eagerly, as if surprised at our safe arrival. The volume of music increased. Several people were weeping. The speaker announced, 'Welcome to Israel'. Teenage girl soldiers with Uzi sub-machine guns waved us out of the aircraft and into buses. The air was palpable, ridiculously warm for a late October afternoon, pressing on our faces, laden with the scent of oranges.

For Rita and me it was our sixth arrival in Israel, but this time we had come to live for an unpredictable period. Jerusalem was no longer a tourist wonder, but home.

The bus wound its way through the Judaean hills as dusk thickened. Road-signs took us gasping into the world of the Bible. Jericho, 40 kilometres. Aialon, 2 kilometres (the valley of Ajalon, where the sun stood still at Joshua's command, see Josh. 10:12-14). Bethshemesh over to the left – yes, where men gathering in the harvest looked up to see the plodding Philistine oxen bringing back the ark of the covenant (1 Sam. 6:13). And where was it kept for a time? At Kiriath Jearim of course (1 Sam. 7:1). We are passing it now, on a steep curve – Kiryat Iarim today. The names hardly change. This is where the Israeli food convoys fought their way up to relieve the starving city in 1948. Bombed and shelled from the steep hillsides, tyres flat and in ribbons, they jolted at 5 m.p.h. for an agonising four hours whilst yelling Arabs ran beside them firing at anyone who moved. Burned-out shells of the vehicles lie by the road, painted annually as a silent memorial to those who died in the attempt.

Arabs died too. Just over to the right again is the desolate ruin of Deir Yassim, at the head of the valley where advancing Philistines were blocked by David's fledgling army. One night in 1948 a Jewish terrorist band massacred the villagers in order to frighten out of the area those who sheltered the convoys' attackers. Another grim tale added to the mythology of Middle East conflict.

Now Jerusalem was in view – perched on the heights, the walls and ramparts aglow in the spotlights. When our grandson first glimpsed it, he shouted, 'Look, there's heaven!'

Not heaven. Not by a long way. And yet mysteriously, mystically holy. So is the whole land. The Holy Land.

But what exactly do we mean by the Holy Land? Why does it exert such a fascination to hundreds of thousands of modern Christians? What can a piece of physical real estate say to us with any claim to be relevant to the gospel at the end of the twentieth century? In fact, its relevance is vital and twofold.

The land fixes the gospel firmly in space and time

There is nothing mythical about the Holy Land. The rocks are solid, the sand is gritty, the water is wet. Nazareth is not in fairyland; it is perched on the stony hills beside the Jezreel valley. Bethlehem is not a scene conjured up for Christmas cards; it is a town on the edge of the Judaean hills. Jerusalem is not an ideal society to be built in England's green and pleasant land; it is 2,000 feet above sea-level on the rising road eastwards from Tel Aviv. You cannot take a taxi or climb off a bus or go for a stroll in Israel without stopping at some physical spot and saying in wonder, 'God did this *here...* it happened *here.'*

This is vital. Not because the places carry some aura of holiness or grace, but because our faith depends on things that God said and did in particular places at a particular time. The gospel is *true,* in the simplest and most basic sense of that word. It is about things that really happened. Some religions depend on myth or symbolic stories which enshrine a mystical truth. Some religions major on cult, their virtue drawn from performing certain rites and ceremonies. But the Christian faith, and indeed the Jewish faith, is committed to fact. God is known by what he is seen to have done. The account of what God did, and his own explanation of why he did it are contained in the Bible. Drawing his certainty from those facts, the Christian says, 'The God who acted for my salvation in the life and death and resurrection of Jesus, can be known by me today. I surrender my will to him and put my trust in him.'

It is vital to say this in today's multi-culture of anything-goes subjectivism. 'Truth is true for you if it works for you – but of course something else works for me.' That is the existentialist argument of today's society, which permeates our literature, art, politics, morality and religion.

'Marriage made up of one man faithful to one woman for life is fine for you, if that's what turns you on. Just don't deny the validity of what turns me on, which is successive passing encounters consummated in different women's beds.'

'Jesus is your Saviour and friend? That's fine. I'm so glad for you. As for me I get my highs from soft drugs, and my friend is switched on to Buddha.'

This is today's atmosphere. In response to it, we need a
message that says rather more than, 'You ask me how I know
he lives? He lives within my heart.' That is certainly true,
and I shall quote examples of its truth. The previous Bishop
of Durham, David Jenkins, would have been perfectly happy
with that – whilst questioning whether Jesus ever came out
of the tomb. But the Jesus who does indeed live in my heart
is the Jesus who lives in objective reality whether or not I
have welcomed him to my heart. He died on a physical cross
for the world's salvation, whether or not any particular person
believes it. He has opened the only way to God, whether or
not some theologians think so. Before him every knee shall
bow, whether or not the rulers of today's world believe it.
The immense reality of Christ, his truth and his salvation in
no way depend on our belief or experience: they are absolute
and objective facts in their own right. *We* don't judge *them*:
they judge *us*.

Living in the Holy Land constantly underlines the fact that
our experience of Christ is based on solid historical fact.
So, for example....

Bethlehem
This is a real place, perched on the long level line of hills
that marks the old Patriarchs' Way, through Shechem, Shiloh,
Bethel, Bethlehem, Hebron and Beersheba: names that vibrate
with biblical associations, yet appear in modern headlines.

Along this line the nomads of the middle bronze era
drifted, their lifestyle now uncovered by archaeology, in a
hundred details that cast light on hitherto obscure and puzzling
Bible stories. Abraham's embarrassing scheme to father a
baby on his wife's personal maid, Jacob's convoluted plots
to grab the birthright, the terror of Joseph's brothers at the

thought of losing their donkeys when they had no qualms about losing their honour... all of these stories reflect the reality of a way of life uniquely fixed in one passing era.

But back to Bethlehem. Heartbroken, Jacob buried his wife Rachel there; the tomb still stands on the right of the Jerusalem-Bethlehem road as it enters the little town (Gen. 35:16-20). Israeli and Palestinian sentries lounge around it, ready to respond to Jewish-Arab rivalries. Ephathrah was its other name, but the source of its more familiar title can be clearly appreciated. 'Bet-Lechem' means 'place of bread'. The rich red soil washed down from the granite hills into Bethlehem's valley make it one of the very places in Judea where barley can be grown with ease. I've walked through the barley fields, deep green in startling contrast to the white sun-bleached slopes. Here, one of the world's great love stories relates, Ruth the Moabitess laboured to glean the sides of the fields as the destitute were allowed to do. Within a choice of only a few acres you can pinpoint the place. Boaz saw her, loved her – and the couple became ancestors of David and ultimately of Jesus.

Where the Philistines fled

Now we can see why young David was sent off to his brothers with food to supplement their army rations (1 Sam. 17). East of Bethlehem, the Elah valley begins to open up, ever widening until it breaks out into the coastal plain near Ashdod. Down there is Philistine country. Those frightening warriors, huge in stature, began to arrive on the coast as Israel appeared out of the desert. They grabbed the rich lowlands from Egypt's control and planted a city at the foot of each river; the famous five cities of Gath, Ashdod, Gaza, Ashkelon and Eglon.

They expanded by the obvious routes, sending raiding

forays up into the heartland of Israel's hill country. Elah is
the broadest and longest valley, thrusting within a few miles
of Bethlehem. It was imperative for Saul's citizen-army to
block the advance here. The point is underscored by the fact
that Israel has a military camp there today, its great radar
saucers pointing towards Philistine land, strung across the
valley at the very point where David confronted Goliath.
The monstrous man makes perfect sense in the story, incidentally. For these Philistines, known to archaeology as 'People
of the Sea', were no less than survivors of the broken Mycenean
Empire whose heroes' exploits were sung by Homer. What
did *they* specialise in? The settlement of battles by personal
one-to-one combat between champions, like Goliath. His
great spear, by the way, was not *the size* of a weaver's beam
(an absurdity) but *as* a weaver's beam – that is with a leather
thong wrapped spirally round it causing it to spin as it was
flung (1 Sam. 17:7). The first rifled bullet, in essence. An
Israelite observer, ignorant of the principle behind it, would
describe it in terms of something he understood.

There really is a stream bed, dry except in the brief winter, scattered with a profusion of 'smooth round stones' (1
Sam. 17:40). Rita and I took so many visiting friends to col-
lect five each, that one day a jeep-load of Israeli soldiers
was sent out from the nearby army camp to ask us what was
going on. A little flustered, I began to explain about David
and Goliath. As soon as I said, 'We are English', they laughed
heartily, shrugged and drove away.

All of these events can be related to known historical
dates, with a convenient date at the beginning of the Iron
Age – say 1000 BC. In fact the Bible account refers to the
immense advantage that Philistines had over Israelites: they
knew how to smelt and work iron (1 Sam. 13:19).

Shepherds and Wise Men

The story leaps a thousand years. Bethlehem becomes the birthplace of Jesus – with immense significance, as an obscure and puzzling prophecy foretells (Mic. 5:1-2; Matt. 2:3-6). The Place of Barley had by now become the centre for a guild of carpenters and stonemasons. Its inhabitants' skills were passed on to their sons. Some emigrated to Galilee in the far north, but still looked to Bethlehem as their centre.

Rome instituted a new custom. The empire increasingly depended on the taxation of conquered countries. In 10 BC Caesar Augustus decreed a systematic census, beginning in Egypt and working northwards into Palestine and Syria. Subjects had to return to their town of origin for registration. It is the factual context for the story of Joseph's return to Bethlehem, his wife heavily pregnant (Luke 2:1-7). News of Jesus' birth was first announced to shepherds, of all people. But it makes perfect sense. Their sheep were, quite specifically in the *fields* (Luke 2:8-9). Sheep were not normally allowed in fields: their place was on the sparsely-grassed stony hills, not on the precious soil where barley could be grown *except* (explains the Talmud) in the winter months between reaping and sowing. And even then, only if they were temple sheep, reared for the sacrifices in the nearby temple in Jerusalem (visible from the heights of Bethlehem).[1] These were no ordinary sheep and no ordinary shepherds. The announcement of the coming of the Lamb of God whose death would bring an end to the sacrificial system was peculiarly appropriate here. There was even a non-biblical tradition which pointed to 'the tower of the shepherds at Bethlehem' as the place at which Messiah would be revealed.

Two miles east of Bethlehem stands the sombre fortress of Herodium. King Herod's slaves built an extraordinary hidden fortress, like the inside of a volcanic crater, by shifting the top half of one hill to the summit of another. Herod the Great – otherwise known as Herod the Butcher – was a great politician, a brilliant architect – and a paranoid tyrant. Not born a Jew himself, and holding the throne (under Rome) by force and flattery, he feared above all else the attention of rivals. That fear drove him to murder his mother, one of his wives, and several of his sons. The naïve question of the magi, 'Where is the one who has been born King of the Jews? We saw his star in the east' (Matt. 2:1-2) threw him into another frenzy of butchery.

There is no independent historical confirmation of the 'massacre of the innocents' in Bethlehem (Matt. 2:16-18). But the story exactly fits what we do know about Herod. The death of perhaps twenty baby boys would, in comparison to some of Herod's crimes, be too small to merit comment outside Bethlehem. Within a few months of that massacre we know that he had another son murdered, for exactly the same reason; his fear of rivals to the throne.

> When Augustus heard that Herod King of the Jews had ordered all the boys in Syria under the age of two years to be put to death and that the King's son was among those killed, he said, 'I'd rather be Herod's *hus* (pig) than Herod's *huios* (son).'[2]

Joseph and Mary fled with the infant Jesus to Egypt. That made sense, because Herod, once a close friend of Cleopatra, had by now fallen out bitterly with Egypt, and built Masada Fortress as part of a defensive network against the south. Nowhere would a child suspected of threatening Herod's throne be more secure from extradition than in Cleopatra's Egypt!

Bethlehem, therefore, serves as a vibrant illustration of

the historicity of Bible events, all of which are underlined
by its geography, geology, botany and history. The land sets
the gospel firmly where God has put it – in the context of
real life, real people, real places and real time. Similar real
people still teach and live that gospel today.... the Palestinian Christians of Bethlehem, some Evangelical and some
Catholic or Orthodox.

There is a second comment to make.

**The land illustrates and encapsulates truth about God
and his people.**
The very climate, topography and vegetation spell out a
theology of One God, rich in mercy. This first dawned on me
when I visited Neot Kedumim. This sprawling 500 acre patch
of ground, the 'Garden of Israel', lies at the foot of the Ajalon
valley. Its purpose is 'to show how the land of Israel became
an inseparable part of the very essence of the Jewish people,
and to explain the significance of this to ... the Bible'.[3]

We bumped over rough tracks in a battered Land Rover.
We tramped over stony hills, splashed across streams, scrambled through scented groves. We lay on our elbows scrib-
bling notes and hunting up Bible references. Every shrub,
flower, tree, grove and terrace held a message. Our Jewish
guide, an agile middle-aged woman was a compendium of
biblical stories and Talmudic lore.

I began to see the whole countryside as an extended parable. 'A land flowing with milk and honey,' our guide said
suddenly. 'Do you know the reference?' She had soon picked
me out as a Christian.

'Yes, of course. Moses' description of the promised land.
Exodus and Deuteronomy.'

Her eyes twinkled. 'Right. Well, what does it *mean*?'

I hesitated. 'Well – a fruitful land, I suppose. A poetic symbol of fruitfulness.'

She laughed. 'All right – but it is literal as well as symbolic. Where do you get milk from?'

'Cows,' I ventured hopefully.

She laughed again. 'Around here it's more likely to be goats. See them over there? Goats grazing on the highlands. Now what about honey? From bees, of course, who get it from the flowers in the lower meadows. So a land flowing with milk and honey is a land of goats and bees in the plentiful grasslands of mountain and meadow. Not like Egypt. Nothing like the wilderness.'

I knew she was teasing me. 'So, what's your point? I'll buy it.'

'You're right: there's more to come. You see, when the Israelites arrived to occupy and settle the land, it ceased to be milk and honey. They ploughed up the meadows for grain and fruit. They terraced the mountain slopes for vineyards. See over here? Milk and honey means rich but uncultivated land. When God gave it to Israel, they changed it. Deuteronomy tells us again. She turned to chapter 8 and read aloud. I joined in from memory, which surprised and pleased her, and scored one point for me. 'The LORD your God is bringing you into a good land – a land with streams and pools of water, with springs flowing in the valleys and hills, a land with wheat and barley, vines and fig trees, pomegranates, olive oil and honey, a land where bread will not be scarce and you will lack nothing' (Deut. 8:7-9).

She snapped the Bible shut. 'Cultivated you see. Milk and honey is the land *waiting to be occupied* and cultivated. Wheat and barley, vine and figs, fruit and olives and date-honey (not bees' honey this time) – that's agriculture in full swing. That's the land *in use* for us.'

She turned to me with a twinkle. 'Right, you know your
Bible. Evangelical Christians do, I've noticed. Better than
Jews, as often as not. So you know about milk and honey in
Exodus and Deuteronomy .... Anywhere else?'

I confessed that she had me stumped.

'Isaiah,' she said tersely. 'Isaiah 7, verses 21-24, to get
the whole sense. The prophet is threatening God's judgement
on a forgetful and disobedient people. Look it up for yourself.'

A fairly masterful type, as Israeli woman often are: I
meekly pulled my Bible out and checked it. 'In that day a
man will keep alive a young cow and two goats. And because of the abundance of the milk they give he will have
curds to eat. All who remain in the land will eat curds and
honey' (Isa. 7:21-22).

I looked up. 'You mean... ?'

'Yes – judgement. The land invaded, the towns destroyed,
the farms burned down, most of the population fled. A few
survivors left, living on what? Milk and honey. The sign of
an empty land, lost again. See what verse 25 says: "As for
all the hills once cultivated by the hoe, you will no longer go
there for fear of the briars and thorns." You see? Back to the
goats and the bees. So to Moses milk and honey meant a gift
from God, ready to be gratefully used. But to Isaiah it meant
the gift taken away again because his people didn't deserve
it, weren't grateful for it, and couldn't keep it.'

Vastly intrigued, I did some research for myself. Winter
evenings in east Jerusalem could be pretty dismal. Rain pat-
tered against the windows, water gurgled down the sloping
drainless streets, the minarets emitted their mournful moans,
the radio only offered an occasional news-bulletin in English, and there was no television. But with a Bible, a con-

cordance, a one-volume commentary and scribbled notes made after conversations with Jewish agriculturalists and Arab shepherds, I had material for fascinating exploration of ideas that made the dark evenings fly.

I went back to those fruits of the land listed by Moses, and recalled the first Sabbath dinner I attended at the University. 'Notice the Seven Fruits on the table,' a student had whispered. I checked rapidly. Loaves made of wheat and barley, wine produced from the vine, a bowl of mixed fruit with figs and pomegranates to the fore, a jar of date honey – but where was the olive oil? My friend nudged me and pointed to the Sabbath Candle, its double wick entwined. 'Candle wax partly made from olive oil,' he whispered. 'Stretching it a bit, I know; it used to be an oil lamp of course. But the idea is there.'

The rabbi intoned verses from the first chapter of Genesis as he broke the loaf open and poured wine gurgling out of the bottle into a cup. Gifts from God the Creator to the world, but a special gift of Jehovah to Israel. 'Be careful that you do not forget,' warned Moses.

I listed the Seven Fruits and began to research their characteristics. And I made a remarkable discovery. As my charming guide at Neot Kedumim could have told me, balance is a very delicate thing in a land which straddles three continents and receives barely enough rain. The most crucial time in the agricultural year is the fifty day period between Passover and Pentecost, that is from mid-April to mid-June. During that period, the flowers of the grape, the pomegranate, the olive and the date all begin to open, and the little embryonic figs begin to develop. At the same time the kernels of the wheat and barley begin to fill out, developing from mere seed to become food.

It is a period when nature holds its breath. Everything depends on certain climatic conditions, but at that time alone, the climate is changeable. Winter sees guaranteed cold and rain (except in a disastrous drought). Summer is hot and dry and can never be anything else. But in Spring, hot *khamsin* sand-winds from the south alternate with cold winds from north and west. The south wind is dry, the north or west breeze brings thunder, lightning, rain. Now, picture the situation. The swelling wheat needs moisture at first: later the rain would destroy it. If the needed rain lasts a few days too long it will damage the opening flowers of the grape, pomegranate, olive and date and prevent them pollinating. On the other hand, if the dry heat comes a few days too soon, the flowers will be happy but the wheat and barley will wither and fail to swell. One feels that it would need a computer to regulate it correctly! No – not a computer, but the Living God, providing for his people in his land. As the Neot Kedumim guide-book explained, 'The Bible underscores that only through a true understanding of the concept of the One Unifying God is it possible to comprehend the balance between the opposing forces which seem to determine the fate of the grain, wine and olive crops.[4]

I began to see the picture. Here is a land where topography and climate, agriculture and economy, domestic life and eating habits all combine in a living parable that bears witness to One God. The great Jewish creed is the *Sh'ma Israel Adonai* – 'Hear O Israel, the LORD your God is one LORD' (Deut. 6:4). Their martyrs have died chanting it, their worshippers have prayed reciting it, their children have been nurtured repeating it. But the Lord says it too, in the very structure, vegetation and climate of the promised land.

Helmut Thielicke, a great preacher of the modern German church, analysing the technique of C. H. Spurgeon, that even greater preacher to Victorian England, sees his secret as the gift of applying the Bible powerfully to the hearers' imagination and conscience.

> When Spurgeon speaks, it is as if the figures of the patriarchs and prophets and apostles were in the auditorium.... You hear the rush of the Jordan and the murmuring of the brook of Siloam, you see the cedars of Lebanon swaying in the wind, hear the clash and tumult of battle between Israel and the Philistines, sense the safety and security of Noah's ark, suffer the agonies of soul endured by Job and Jeremiah, hear the creak of oars as the disciples strain against the contrary winds, and feel the dread of the terrors of the apocalypse.... The heart is so full of scripture, that it leavens the consciousness, peoples the imagination with its images, and determines the landscape of the soul by its climate.[5]

Now what the Bible did in Spurgeon's hands through God-anointed preaching, the Bible does in the hands of someone walking through modern Israel when the same Spirit is at work. Then the land does indeed 'make the ubiquity of the Scriptures a real and living fact'. There is nothing automatic about it. But to the visitor whose senses are sharpened by faith, the whisper of God comes clearly.

It is this that makes Israel-Palestine truly 'the Holy Land'.

References

1. *The Talmud.* Menahot 97a, Hagiga 27a.
2. Raymond E Brown, *The Birth of the Messiah*, Cassell, 1993, p. 226.
3. Nogah Hareuveni, *Nature in our Biblical Heritage,* Neot Kedumim Ltd, Israel, 1980, translated from the Hebrew.
4. Nogah Hareuveni, *Ibid* p. 43.
5. Helmut Thielicke, *Encounter with Spurgeon,* translated by John Deberstein (James Clarke & Co. Ltd., 1964), p. 9.

2

Moonscape and Legends

Is there anywhere else quite like the Dead Sea basin? I doubt it. A great chasm in the earth cuts Israel off from its eastern neighbours and encloses the silent sinister sea that symbolises man's sin and God's judgement.

There it lies, as you come to the edge of the Judaean desert. You can scramble downhill from ancient Arad and its modern settlers' city, or take a taxi down the twisting road from Jerusalem to Jericho, made world-famous by the parable of the Good Samaritan. Sullen, oily and dull when seen close-to, the sea appears brilliant turquoise from a distance; an immense artificial swimming pool superimposed incongruously upon the grim, moonlike landscape.

Fifty-five miles long, ten miles wide, and a startling 1,300 feet deep in places, it has another very great oddity. The shore and surface is over 1,200 feet below sea level. Israeli guides will often enjoy their little joke as they bring their tourists down past the Inn of the Good Samaritan, and stop the bus at the first vantage-point of the plain below. 'Please slide your windows shut – we are about to drop below sea-level,' they say straight faced. Usually someone will do it anxiously peering out to see if the water is seeping in!

Great limestone cliffs, seamed with fissures and riddled with caves, fall in a curtain of rock, a thousand feet at a time, or in hundred-foot steps, to the barren shores of this strange stretch of water around which legend and Bible history, discovery and terror have gathered.

Here the grim judgement fell on vicious sensual cities of
the middle bronze era known inside and outside of the Bible
as the Cities of the Plain. Abraham's nephew Lot escaped
after receiving warnings from angels, but Lot's wife looked
back and was engulfed. Next day Abraham gazed down from
the Judaean hills, 'and he saw dense smoke rising from the
land, like smoke from a furnace' (Gen. 19:28).

Nature and history, topography and chemistry, theology
and scenery uniquely combine to illustrate and expound this
awful drama of divine judgement on human wickedness. The
very words sin, Sodom and Siddim conspire in onomato-
poeic agreement. The empty precipices seem to symbolise
desolation and forsakenness, suggestive of the very edges of
hell, whilst the shimmering heat of the vast hollow, the desolate salt-pans, the grotesque rock formations and the linger-
ing smell of sulphur all combine to turn long-past tales of
judgement into daily warning that the wages of sin is death.

The Bible treats the Genesis story both literally and sym-
bolically. Clearly the overthrow of the Cities of the Plain is
meant to be understood as a literal event. Airy attempts of
liberal scholars and theologians to dismiss it as a typical
legend, expressing subconscious race-characteristics fall flat
on their faces, tripped over by the facts. Myths of fire from
heaven and cities buried beneath the sea are indeed a common phenomenon. But in sober fact, the Bible never suggests for one moment that the doomed cities are below the
sea in Atlantis-like ruin. Genesis describes burning sulphur
raining from the skies, the cities 'overthrown' and the vegetation permanently destroyed, 'and smoke covering the land'
(Gen. 19:23-28).

Earlier incidents during the same generation suggest an
odd juxtaposition of fertile attractive land, populous towns,

and a desolate and dangerous area full of tar-pits (Gen. 13:10; 14:10). The land is clearly volcanic but something less than an erupting volcano would be sufficient to match the description. Similar districts in America have seen cataclysms as a result of oil and gas pockets building up pressure until they burst through the rock and spurt burning oil into the sky, mingled with salt, sulphur and mud.

What happened to Lot's wife was not a kind of magic spell turning her into a pillar of salt in fairytale style (as children and even their teachers sometimes imagine). Lot was shamefully reluctant to leave the doomed city where he had settled in comfort and spoiled his witness to God (Gen. 19:18-20). His wife was even slower to take warning, and lingered short of the safety of the mountains, hanging back to sorrow over the loss of her sadly-compromised home. The convulsion overtook her, as they had been warned it might: 'Flee for your lives! Don't look back, and don't stop anywhere in the plain! Flee to the mountains or you will be swept away!'

Presumably she was caught and overwhelmed by the horrific burning mixture from the sky, which immediately cooled and hardened, so that where she lingered there now stood 'a pillar of salt' (Gen. 19:26). Guides today will obligingly point out solitary rocky pillars standing amidst the flat, featureless, sulphur-smelling salt-pans south-west of the sea; some of them bear an eerie resemblance to a figure hesitating and peering over its shoulder. Unfortunately, they would make the wretched woman between fifteen and twenty-five feet high!

The whole story of the overthrow of the cities offers a classic example of the principles that lie behind that most disliked and reviled truth that *God punishes sin.* The facts

are all there. Sin is not merely against my neighbour but
'*against God*' (13:13). The almighty Judge examines men's
behaviour: 'I will go down and see' (18:21) carries the sense
of arranging a trial and mustering the evidence. God is reluctant to punish and eager to forgive if there is penitence, and
his verdict is always just: 'Will not the Judge of all the earth
do right?' (18:25).

God's people have a role to play in intercessory prayer
(note the remarkable dialogue between Abraham and God,
18:22-33). Where there is the slightest hope of a change of
heart, God will delay judgement, send warnings and offer a
way of escape (19:12-13).

However, not only is this incident literally true, it also
holds symbolic significance. Its warning is reinforced and
applied by Moses (Deut. 29:23), by Amos (4:11), by Isaiah
(1:9) and by Jeremiah (23:14). Jesus turned the story inside
out: the fate of the cities of Galilee to which he preached
will be worse than that of Sodom and Gomorrah because
these cities have seen and rejected more light, heard more
truth and witnessed more evidence of the love and holiness
of God (Matt. 10:15; 11:20-24). New Testament writers Paul,
Peter and Jude all refer to it (Rom. 9:29; 2 Pet. 2:6; Jude 7).
The last book in the Bible takes up the theme again, and in
stunning symbolism combines pictures of Pharaoh's Egypt,
Lot's Sodom, the Jerusalem that crucified Christ, and the
whole God-rejecting world-system as the great city, which
is figuratively Sodom and Egypt, where also their Lord was
crucified (Rev. 11:8).

Fact and Fantasy
Water runs into the Dead Sea but cannot run out again. There
it lies, steaming under the burning sun, the effect heightened

by sea haze that hangs more densely over this place than any other on earth. The waters running in from the surrounding mountains carry the usual mineral salts and more – for they run through nitrous soil and are fed by sulphuric springs. The water evaporates in the intense heat, forming a quivering translucent haze. The minerals are left behind, in ever-increasing volume. The water of an average ocean (bitter enough to our taste) contains 4-6% solids in solution. In the Dead Sea it is an astonishing 32%.

A liquid that is one-third solid is going to have some odd properties! No wonder strange stories abound throughout history. The *Yam Hamelach,* the Salt Sea, was its ancient name (Gen. 14:3). Aristotle told Alexander the Great that no fish lived in its mysterious depths, and that a body cast on its waters will float forever. When the Roman Emperor Vespasian arrived with his conquering army he heard strange tales of slaves who had escaped by running across its waters whilst their frightened pursuers shrank back. With the callous indifference to human suffering of a tyrant, he ordered that anyone who could not swim should be thrown in with their hands bound behind their backs. They floated. So may the modern visitor, if he wishes.

You can go home with the statutory snapshot of yourself reading a newspaper whilst lying on the water. You cannot actually swim because you float, your stomach about three inches below the surface, your back exposed, and your progress maintained by splashing and lurching along like a hippopotamus stranded on a submerged sandbank.

These bemusing characteristics have led to a stream of travellers' tales, superstitions and ridiculous exaggeration that mingle fact and fantasy. Clothes become instantly clean by immersing them in Dead Sea waters. Birds venturing to

fly across its surface instantly drop dead. Its water holds
marvellous medicinal powers, and is bottled and sold in
Rome. Monsters lurk in its depths. It covers the mouth of
hell. Jewish historian Josephus picturesquely described the
sea 'coughing up black asphalt chunks that float on the water, looking like headless oxen'. The cursed cities of Sodom
and Gomorrah lurked below the waters, still exercising a
malign influence. So they say.

Early explorers
Consequently, until the nineteenth century the whole area was
feared and shunned. Nothing factual was known about it.
The first modern explorers only enhanced its mysterious and
malign reputation. Ulrich Seelzen, a German adventurer, arrived in 1806, having gone to the elaborate lengths of living
in Syria for four years and converting to Islam, disguised
himself first as an Arab and then a Greek Orthodox monk.
He stuck to the eastern shore, mapped it carefully and discovered Herod's fortress of Machaerus where John the Baptist was beheaded. He could find no trace of the huge supplies of asphalt to which both Bible and travellers' tales
bore witness. They were awaiting discovery on the western
side.

The first attempt to sail the waters combined elements of
romance, eccentricity and tragedy. Christopher Costigan, a
young Irishman, brought a small boat with him from Europe,
met up with a Maltese sailor, mastered the art of sailing the
craft on Galilee and the upper stretches of Jordan, then transported it overland to the Dead Sea. The frail craft zigzagged
across the sullen sea, its tiny crew ill-equipped and scien-
tifically naive. They took observations and measurements,
bailed out the constantly-leaking boat and drank coffee made

from the salt-laden water. It was August, with the heat at its most merciless, and Costigan went out of his mind, claiming to see the ruins of Gomorrah in the depths. The nameless Maltese sailor left the Irishman with Bedouins near Jericho and walked to Jerusalem for help. It came too late: Costigan died of fever, heat-exhaustion and dehydration.

There was a morbid and curious sequel. A few months afterwards, John Stephens, American pioneer of Middle Eastern exploration, found Costigan's abandoned boat now constituting one wall of a hut in which he was sleeping at Jericho. He tracked down the Maltese, obtained the maps drawn on the ill-fated voyage, and published them. The mystical fantasy-sea was taking on clear shape. Almost immediately another German explorer, Von Schubert, hit on one of the scientific secrets behind the myths. Taking daily measurements of air temperature and barometric pressure, he suddenly began to find absurd readings which suggested that the sea was below sea-level! Clearly the instrument was broken. But as soon as he left the area, it seemed to mend itself. The truth dawned.

Along came the English. Lieutenant Thomas Molyneux from *HMS Spartan* stationed at Haifa, transported a ship's boat to the area and sailed south from the exit of Jordan. Beset first by frightening storms, the waves striking the boat as if they were solid objects, and then by flat calms when the crew had to row and bail constantly in the gasping heat, they mapped out a wavering course but had to give up.

It was high time that good old American know-how took a hand and tackled the thing professionally. In 1857 a complete expeditionary force from the US Navy brought three specially constructed boats under the command of Captain William Francis Lynch. They spent a month mapping, measuring, collecting specimens, drawing sketches, noting winds and currents and recording temperatures, weather conditions and atmospheric pressures.

Science had arrived. The days of mystery were over, or so it seemed. But undreamed-of secrets were still to be unlocked.

3

Secrets of the Dead Sea

One torrid day in 1947 a Bedouin shepherd-boy, grazing his goats along the north-western shore of the Dead Sea, made a discovery which shook the archaeological world and brought the area into the newspaper headlines of a hundred countries. One of the goats scrambled into a cave part-way up a steep slope. The lad shouted, whistled, and lobbed a stone into the gloom. He heard a splintering noise. His missile had broken one of a row of large sealed clay pots hidden in the cave. The Dead Sea Scrolls were about to burst on an astonished world.

The pots (it eventually became clear) had stood there ever since some frightened scribe had hidden them from the grim advance of the Roman legions in their bid for a final solution to the problem of the Jews. No doubt he had hopes of retrieving them. It would have been beyond his power to imagine that they would stand there in the hot dry gloom for almost 1,900 years.

Hidden from the Romans, then rediscovered in a day of automobiles, aeroplanes, space-flight and nuclear fission – but what was in the jars? The contents proved to be a mini-library of ancient documents written painstakingly on animal skins sewn together and rolled into scrolls.

The story of how the scrolls eventually came into the hands of Israeli scholars is a drama in itself, comparable to *King Solomon's Mines* or *Raiders of the Lost Ark*. The area, at

that time, was still part of the Kingdom of Jordan. The newly-
created state of Israel was under attack from Jordan and ten
other Arab nations, and fighting desperately for its life. A
famous Israeli archaeologist visited Arab Bethlehem on a
public bus, bought three scrolls from a Greek antique-dealer,
and smuggled them out under his shirt whilst snipers' bullets
hummed past. Four other documents were illegally flown
out of Jordan to America by a Christian priest who was determined to raise money from them for his war-stricken or-
phanage. Secret meetings with an Israeli cabinet minister
led to their purchase for many times the price the monk had
paid – and their surreptitious journey back across the Atlan-
tic to Jerusalem. Others (including the fabulous Temple
Scroll) took fifteen years to travel around the world and
were tracked down via clues picked up in Moscow and in
the Wall Street Journal. When, in 1967, the Israeli forces
poured down the Mount of Olives and captured the ancient
walled city of Jerusalem, a high-ranking minister was minutes behind the advance guard who stormed into the
Rockefeller Museum outside Herod Gate. He courteously
advised startled scholars still examining other scrolls that
they now belonged to Israel, who would hold them in trust
for the whole world of scholarship.

When, as a result of the same June war, the whole of the
western shore of the Dead Sea was 'liberated' (as Israelis
always express it), the army, the scholars and the politicians
combined in scroll-hunting task-forces to hunt through thousands of caves. Little more from the first century turned up,
but another half-mythical page of Jewish history was uncovered by the discovery of letters and relics of the Bar Kokhba
rebellion of 150 AD when the freedom fighters actually re-
occupied ruined Jerusalem for two years.

What did it all add up to?

One blazing April day I trudged across the sand-strewn rocks and scrambled up to the original cave where it all began. Looking down from it, I could see laid out before me the ruins of the Qumran Community, pinpointed and excavated from the clues provided by the scrolls. For these mysterious documents came from what was probably the library of the Essenes – a group of Jewish religious enthusiasts not mentioned in the Bible, but described by Jewish and pagan writers in terms that had often led to the suspicion that they never really existed.

But they had existed. Stern, ascetic, passionately committed to the Law and the Prophets, led by a vaguely sketched figure called the Teacher of Righteousness, they planted their monastic community in this wild and solitary place. And their library? It contained precious copies of whole sections of the Old Testament (older by a thousand years than anything that Jew or Christian so far possessed). There were commentaries on Bible passages too: fascinating insight into the way they read and interpreted the Scriptures. Their own *Book of Discipline* threw a flood of light on the principles and practices of the community. A strange book, *The War of the Sons of Light Against the Sons of Darkness*, bears some resemblance to the books of Daniel and Revelation. Here were other fascinating books – pious creations from the time between Old and New Testament, used by both Jews and early Christians, and including the Book of Enoch, for example which Jude 14 quotes but which had been lost to history.[1]

Qumran and the Christians

I stood beside one of the five 'baptistries' in the ruins of the
Community as one of Jerusalem's top scholars lectured. Later
we examined the awesome Isaiah scroll, preserved in the
Dome of the Scrolls opposite Israel's parliament in Jerusalem – page after page sewn together vertically and occupy-
ing an entire curved wall.

What does it all really tell us about early Christianity?

At first there were the wildest rumours. Qumran was John
the Baptist's headquarters. The feet of Jesus had walked these
corridors. Jesus was brought up here as a child. 'The Teacher
of Righteousness' was either John the Baptist or Jesus. The
apostles borrowed their teaching from the Essenes. The Bible was variously proved to be 'true' and 'untrue'. The whole
of early Church history would have to be rewritten. And so
on. Writers of fast selling and quickly forgotten religious
speculations had a field-day.

Most of this was greatly exaggerated. The facts, simply,
are these. The Jewish world of Jesus' time was rather more
complicated than we had imagined. It was an era of great
creativity and original thought, of excitement, expectation
and fanaticism. The Essenes were dissatisfied with the Pharisees who interpreted the Law and the Sadducees who ran
the Temple priesthood – and for pretty much the same reason as Jesus condemned those two groups. But the Essenes'
reaction took them further away from Jesus not closer to
him. In their extreme other-worldliness they regarded the
narrow-minded Pharisees as careless libertines! What they
would have thought of Jesus, with his emphasis on inner
cleanliness rather than religious performance, defies the imagination!

We already know that Jews 'baptised' (plunged into a

mikvah or ritual bath) Gentiles who were converted to their faith. They also had ritual purification for various situations (after childbirth, for example). Essenes took the thing further, and had ritual immersion for *themselves,* probably repeated every day.

The Essenes longed for the coming Messiah and saw themselves as fulfilling the vision of Isaiah 40:3. 'A voice of one calling: In the desert prepare the way for the LORD, in the wilderness make straight a highway for our God.'

Here there is an overlap with the New Testament story. It seems evident now that not only the Essenes lived in the wilderness of Judaea. Thousands of people influenced by them but not prepared to join them, went on short-term pilgrimages to camp in the wilds and prepare themselves for God's Kingdom. John the Baptist went there – not only calling crowds to come out and hear him, but going there himself because that's where the crowds were – and no doubt attracting more by his presence: 'In those days John the Baptist came, preaching in the desert of Judaea and saying, "Repent, for the Kingdom of heaven is near"' (and Matthew then quotes the above Isaiah prophecy).

John's baptism, of course, was not a daily ritual cleansing but a once-for-all confession of sin leading to a change of heart and attitude – as his instructions made clear (Luke 3:7-14).

Speaking into the situation

Fascinating light, then, on the beginning of Jesus' ministry. He spoke into a situation ripe for his message. The wording of that message, too, has some bearing on Qumran. Readers of the New Testament have often commented on the striking difference between Jesus' reported 'style' as recorded in

John's Gospel on the one hand, and Matthew, Mark and Luke on the other. Instead of simple workaday parables of the Kingdom there are strongly theological, technical, almost abstract themes.

Light and Darkness, Truth and Error, Life and Death: these are the subjects related by John. Why the difference? Some scholars have too hastily claimed an irreconcilable contradiction. 'This language of light and life and truth is not first century Jewish at all,' they have told us. 'This is the speech of second-century Greek thinking. John's Gospel has nothing to do with John the fisherman or Jesus the Galilee rabbi. Some second-century Christian writer (perhaps in Ephesus) has "worked up" some of the Jesus miracle-stories and put onto the lips of Jesus his own profound meditations on their meaning.'

The scrolls give the dramatic lie to that. For some of them are full of John's kind of language and they are firmly dated as early first-century Jewish writings from the vicinity of Jerusalem. What presumably happened was that Jesus, the master-communicator, adapted his language to the thought-forms and themes current around Jerusalem (where most of John's narrative is set), just as in Galilee he used the familiar scenes of Galilean life, in Samaria he took up a woman on a subject that greatly excited the Samaritans, and when facing the temple priests and teachers, argued in their own idiom.

Of course what Jesus actually *taught* was totally different from the doctrine of the Essenes. Far from being a development of their system, Christianity offered a drastic alternative.

I sometimes talked to a highly articulate bishop of an ancient church, who lived on the Mount of Olives. The 'Church

of the East' claims an unbroken line back to the early Nazarene Christians of Galilee. Although its present membership
is largely Arab, its character is rather Jewish. They observe
the Passover, for example, and their liturgical language is a
development of the Aramaic which Jesus presumably spoke.

The bishop assured me that disillusioned survivors of the
disbanded Essenes were converted to Christianity after the
destruction of Jerusalem (at the time when the scrolls were
hidden). The failure of their expectations must have been
painful. Rigid law-keeping (and more than the law required)
had not brought the Messiah. The Children of Light had *not*
overcome the Children of Darkness (the Romans) in war –
just the opposite. How ripe they must have been for a Messiah who changes the inward nature, a kingdom that is not of
this world, a conquest of sin and death won by one who died
on a Roman cross, a baptism that spoke not of ritual require-
ments but of the passage from spiritual death to new life!

References

1. For Dead Sea Scrolls, see Yigael Yadin, *The Message of the Scrolls*,
Touchstone, USA, 1957. Geza Vermes, *The Dead Sea Scrolls in
English*, SCM, 1987.

4

Prophets, Priests and Poets

The guide's English was usually good, but this time he got it slightly wrong. 'To picture the land, think of a skeleton running down the middle,' he said to his bemused bus passengers. 'He means a *spine*,' I whispered.

That is indeed a helpful way to picture the topography. Imagine three broad north-south strips of land running parallel. Each varies from 10 to 30 miles across, usually widening as we move south. The central strip is the mountainous spine.

First on the left (west) is the Mediterranean Coastal Strip. Flat, sandy, well watered and warm, it supports the fruitful citrus orchards of the new State of Israel. Here the returning Zionists waded secretly ashore, sometimes with guns thrust into their hands as they scrambled through the surf, whilst the more legal 'quotas' alighted from ships at Haifa. Tel Aviv with its jumble of smart skyscrapers and gimcrack prefabs now sprawls along 25 miles of the sea front, linking other modern towns and holiday resorts like Bat Yam, Herzlia and Natanya.

We are driving northwards on the route of the ancient 'Via Maris', the Way of the Sea, classic route from Pharaoh's Egypt to Syria. The crowded modern highway with the sea always in sight is Israel's M1.

Inland, on our right, is the great mountain range, by far the broadest and most dominant feature of the land, and the one that is so gratifyingly 'biblical'. The long, gradual slope is the westward sea-facing side. On average it takes 25 miles to rise 2,000 feet. Sloping moorland breaks into scalps and ridges of rock. Shallow shadowed valleys contrast with the white sunlit surfaces to create an odd effect, not only of three dimensions, but of four. This slope is the biblical *Shephelah* of Scripture, Apocrypha and Talmud.[1] Variously translated Hill Country, Lowlands or Foothills, it provided the theatre on which much of the drama of the Old and New Testaments was acted out. Here was the debated ground between Israelite and Philistine, between Maccabee and Syrian, between Crusader and Muslim. Today the dispute is between Jewish settler and Palestinian native.

Many biblical place-names have only changed a little, especially in Arabic; a fact that enabled the great Protestant Victorian explorers to identify and 'recover' them. Today one can engage in a geographical treasure-hunt, Bible and map at the ready, tracking down the scenes of one event after another in the fortunes of Samson and David in the south, Joshua and Samuel in the east, Elijah and Elisha in the centre and north.

This is the Judaea and Samaria of biblical times; the southern and northern Kingdoms respectively after the disruption following Solomon's death. Rather confusingly to us, the *land* was then called Judaea and Samaria, but the *kingdoms* were named Judah and Israel. Two centuries later, Israel collapsed and its population was deported by the Assyrians. They were forcibly replaced by the racially mixed Samaritans whom we meet again in Jesus' time. Nowadays, much of Samaria is Palestinian 'West Bank', occupied by modern Israel in 1967, and now being gradually relinquished; the focus of world media interest, as Jewish settlers and Palestinian populace live in uneasy and sometimes violent juxtaposition. It is still the Debated Land.

So much for the western slope of the mountain spine. On its eastern side it drops steeply and dramatically, from 2-3,000 feet *above* sea level, down to 800-1300 *below*. At its highest points (travelling from south to north, once more) stand Hebron, Bethlehem, Jerusalem, Ramallah and Nablus.

All throb with biblical echoes. It was in Hebron that Abraham bought a cave in which to bury his beloved wife (Gen. 23). The spot is both a synagogue and a mosque today. Grim-faced Israeli soldiers and Palestinian Police keep the rival religionists apart.

Nablus at the northern end of the spine is the biblical Shechem, sprawling over the slopes of Mount Ebal. Here, in the natural amphitheatre between mounts Ebal and Gerizim, Joshua solemnly gathered the invading Israelites to re-dedicate themselves to God (Josh. 8:30-35). Archaeologists believe they have recently found the memorial pillar that Joshua raised. At Shechem, too, can be found the well dug out by Jacob, at which, a thousand years later Jesus had that conversation with 'a woman of Samaria' which drew out such sublime truths (John 4). Rita and I stopped to drink from it, on one of our rare and perhaps rash visits (for tension is always high here). As a Greek Orthodox priest drew the water for us we saw that indeed 'the well is deep' (verse 11); 115 feet deep in fact! No need to wonder whether this is the very place; unbroken tradition has cherished its memory, and there are no alternative choices in this dry land. Successive Christian buildings have stood there since the late fourth century.

Finally, in our sketch of the three parallel regions, is that deep natural ditch that runs from Galilee in the north to the Great Lakes of central Africa in the south; the Great Rift. Within the Holy Land itself, it forms the Jordan Valley. This biblical river, the land's only major water supply, emerges at three

points from Hermon's range in Lebanon, widens briefly to
form Lake Galilee, narrows again and meanders southward
past Jericho, and empties into the Dead Sea.

George Adam Smith, one of the Victorian topographers,
waxed understandably eloquent at the sight of this stream.

> There may be something on the surface of another planet to match
> the Jordan Valley: there is nothing on this.... There are hundreds of
> streams more large, more useful, or more beautiful; there is none
> which has been more spoken about by mankind .... to half the world,
> the short, thin thread of the Jordan is the symbol of both great fron-
> tiers of the spirit's life on earth – the baptism through which it passes
> into God's Church, and the waters of death which divide this pilgrim
> fellowship from the promised land.[2]

Joshua and his army crossed with the sacred ark. Elijah struck
the waters with his cloak. Elisha sent the leprous Naaman to
wash and be healed. John baptized penitents. The holy dove
descended upon Jesus. The Saviour's long journey to the cross
took him along the eastern bank through Decapolis and Peraea,
as recorded by Luke. Ample reasons for Jordan's eternal cel-
ebration.

Climate and Conscience

There is a simple way to understand the link between weather
and topography. Memorise this rule: 'East is dry, west is wet.'
Then add another: 'South is hot, north is cool.' That is a rough
guide in England, but much more absolute and extreme in Israel.
Rain comes in from the Mediterranean and precipitates on the
west-facing slopes that it reaches first. Eastern slopes face the
sun all day, baking in its heat. Cold air comes from the north, hot
desert winds blow from the eastern and southern deserts.

Now add another rule: 'the deeper, the hotter.' The great
crevasse of Jordan, 20 miles wide, falls ever further below

sea-level as the river winds southwards. From the heights above, it resembles a great winding green snake, crawling between banks of white marl, clusters of dark tamarisks and tangled tropical bush. Heat haze often obscures the view. Modern Israeli and Palestinian farmers are gradually claiming the area for agriculture, and an added oddity today is the sight of acres of glass and plastic cloches that look from a distance like sun reflecting on water.

Needless to say, life has always been tougher and more demanding in the hot dry east and south, than in the bracing well-watered west and north. Life on the edge of the desert is harsh, simple, nomadic. There is neither time nor opportunity for the pursuit of luxury. The sun blazes down; searching, scorching, purifying.

Is it mere coincidence that the Israelites arrived, with their stern commandments and holy covenant from the *east* and *south*? Elijah appears abruptly to warn the northern court of the corrupting influence of Phoenician Baal-worship from further west and north, and he retreats south and east for spiritual refreshment. Amos is a shepherd in the stony dry heights, who gets extra work in-season by helping with the sycamore-fig harvest. Called by God to warn and prophesy, he travels north and west to Samaria (1 Kgs. 17-19; Amos 7: 10-17).

For just as the very topography and climate of south and east etch on the consciousness the call to simplicity and holiness, so the easier conditions of north and west offer more ease, more prosperity, more leisure to get up to mischief. And those sophisticated coastal cities are closer, with their Caananite idolatry and their moral corruption. It is on the slopes of western sea-coast Carmel that Elijah battles for Israel's soul with the Baalites from nearby Phoenicia (1 Kgs. 17). It is in the northern capital of Samaria that Amos derides luxury-loving city women as 'cows of Bashan', and condemns men for spending wealth on imported ivory furniture, whilst God's poor go hungry (Amos 4:1; 5:11; 6:4). Even Jesus' forerunner John lives in the eastern 'wilderness', and gathers around him people from the cities to prepare for a baptism of fire (Matt. 3:1-12).

The Sound of Truth

The very language of the Holy Land carries a phonetic message, too. Hebrew, the language of the Jewish Bible, has been rediscovered and restored, in a manner unprecedented in human history. Once so disused that no-one knew how to pronounce it, Hebrew is now Israel's language again. Its liquid beauty, with the accent so often on the final syllable, somehow *sounds* right; poetic, appealing, yet decisive, as if God himself is both inviting and commanding through it.

Many biblical passages present propositional truth (declarations of fact that require our assent and submission). But many more offer the language of Hebrew metaphor, symbol, idiom, story and picture. Consider the commonest words used to describe God's people; they are garden, vineyard, sheepfold and city. All involve oriental metaphor, not logical Latin propositions. The Hebrew Bible is more a work of literature than of systematic doctrine. Its theology and ethics are expressed in poems 'about the weather, trees, crops, lions, hunters, rocks of refuge and human emotions such as love and terror and trust and joy'.[3]

This realisation is crucial to a right interpretation of Scripture, and unwary westerners, over-dependent on Latin logic, can easily stray. Contrast Isaiah's visions of God (or John's prologue, for that matter) with the Athanasian Creed

or the Westminster Confession! Poetry and metaphor appeal
to imagination and emotion rather than reason and logic. On
the other hand, the emotion needs to be *informed*. What did
a city, a sheepfold or a garden mean *in their Middle-Eastern
context?* To us a city suggests urban sprawl and sophisticated
living and social inequality. An ancient city was, by
definition, a settlement with a protective wall around it; the
connotations suggested security and community!

As a child in an English industrial town, I 'knew' the
twenty-third psalm, but entertained grotesque mental images of what it meant. I pictured myself seated at a table
which stood in a field of rich grass beside a stream. The
cloth was laid with utensils and loaded with food of the
children's party variety; jelly, chocolate cake and suchlike.
Peering round nearby bushes were the scowling faces of
human 'enemies' (school bullies and German soldiers). A
cloth-capped sheep farmer, familiar in Stockton cattle-mar-
ket, poured brylcream hair-oil on my head and combed my
hair. Yet in spite of this confusion, the basic 'meaning' somehow still got across; God gives provision and protection to
those who relate to him in trustful obedience. Of course I
did not word it that way, but I felt it. Poetry appeals to the
imagination rather than the logical faculty.

Living in Israel and Palestine where the biblical metaphors
originated, I had fascinating talks with a Palestinian olive-
farmer, a Bedouin shepherd, a Melkite priest whose church
members could trace direct if very mixed descent from the
Galilee of Jesus time, and an American scholar who immersed
himself in village life almost unchanged for three thousand
years. The conversations threw floods of light on the language
and meaning of the Bible.

Here is another irony; one learns more about the *culture*

of Bible times from Arabs than from Jews. The Palestinian peasant follows customs little changed from David's Judaea or Peter's Galilee. The Israeli, on the hand, is more likely to come from America, Poland or Russia, bringing with him twentieth or nineteenth-century customs and sophisticated attitudes. A Palestinian will farm olives almost exactly as Israelites did twenty-five hundred years ago; his Jewish counterpart will explain to you how to cultivate genetically engineered oranges designed to grow at a consistent height of two metres to be picked by machine !

Consider that image of the vine and vineyard as a metaphor for God's people. The detailed picture in Isaiah 5 practically explains itself. So does Jesus' parable of the rebellious vineyard tenants, which takes the symbol a logical step further (Matt. 21: 33-46). But his startling allegory in John 15 switches the emphasis from Israel's corporate calling to the individual Christian's personal walk with Christ, and some of the teaching depends heavily on the reader's understanding of vine cultivation.

The leaves near the ground are 'lifted up' and held in little cleft twigs to keep them out of the damp dust and mildew ('cut off' is an unfortunate and unlikely translation). Branches are pruned to avoid over-luxuriant and fruitless growth. The crop is gently washed in water. All of this (recorded in verses 1-4) has searching application to our personal devotional life. The branches that are thrown into the fire and burned (verse 6) do not provide a warning of hell. You will find along the roadside today, unfruitful and withered branches gathered to fulfil a secondary use; they provide fuel; valuable, but not fulfilling their best potential. In modern Bethlehem they find a further subsidiary use as carved models, sold to tourists and pilgrims.

Picture and Parables

Needless to say, the parables of Jesus reflected a context of custom and culture. I walked with that scholar from the Arab villages as we discussed this. *Story* was and is the supreme Oriental medium of truth. Although the parables had unique features about them, they were nevertheless *stories*, and as such were familiar and welcome. They reflected a world familiar to their first hearers, but then turned it upside down with the paradoxes of grace – like the casual labourers who get a day's pay for an hour's work.

Take the story of the man who wakens his neighbour at midnight to ask for three loaves to feed an unexpected guest (Luke 11). It was a familiar scenario. Within the solidarity of a small village (Nazareth's population would be around 200, most of them inter-related) anyone's visitor was a guest of the community. Hospitality was a sacred obligation. A traveller turned away might easily die. It was assumed that neighbours would pool their resources; to refuse to do so was unthinkable. Jesus poses a humorous question: 'Can you *imagine* a man who is asked for help *refusing*, with ridiculous chatter about the family in bed?'

'No, of course not,' would be the laughing reply, 'that is unthinkable!'

'Just so,' implies Jesus. 'And how much more unthinkable that God should ignore the prayers of his people, especially when help to others and the honour of the (church) community are involved.'

The point of the story is not the persistent asking of the petitioner (refusal is inconceivable). The 'without shame' of verse 8, misunderstood by western readers as shameless begging, refers to the unshamed honour of the awakened householder, who for his reputation's sake and that of the village, cannot and will not refuse. God's glory is at stake in his answering of prayer.

We have strayed now from Old to New Testament, but that is not surprising. 'The New is in the Old concealed; the Old is in the New revealed.' The land of sheep and vines, of walled villages and excavated wells, of terraced hills and corn-filled valleys, of farmers and soldiers .... is the land of prophets, priests and poets who prepared the way for the coming Christ who is God's *Yes* to all of his own promises (2 Cor. 1:19-20).

References

1. Neither ancient writings nor modern maps are uniformly consistent in the references to the Shephelah, as a professor at the Hebrew University explained to me. Certainly Luke regarded it as the whole mossif, not just the lower western slopes (Luke 1:39-40).

2. George Adam Smith, *The Historical Geography of the Holy Land*, Hodder & Stoughton, 1894, pp. 467-8.

3. L. Ryken, *Triumphs of the Imagination*, IVP, USA 1979, p. 22, quoted by John Goldingay, *Models For Scripture*, Eerdmans, 1994, p. 314. Both authors are engaged in exploring the implications of biblical inspiration and interpretation.

Part Two

The City

Below the spare slopes of the Mount of Olives runs the Valley of Jehoshophat, to which the trumpets of the Last Judgment will call the souls of all mankind.... Generations of Christians, Jews and Moslems sleep scattered under a sea of whitened stone, achieving in death in Jerusalem what they had so often failed to achieve in life: a peaceful reconciliation of their claims to its ramparts (Larry Collins & Dominique Lapieroc, *O Jerusalem!*).

> Walk about Zion, go round her,
> count her towers,
> consider well her ramparts,
> view her citadels
> that you may tell of them to the next generation.
> (Psalm 48:12-13)

> Jerusalem, Jerusalem... how often I have longed to gather
> your children together... but you were not willing
> (Matthew 23:37).

5

Four Quarters Make One History

Ten measures of beauty descended to the world. Nine were taken by Jerusalem – and one by the rest of the world. So says the Talmud.[1] An exaggeration, but a pardonable one. It can look breathtaking as you drive up over the wooded rocky hummocks of Judea, and suddenly see it, the golden limestone shining, the walls and ramparts in fairytale profusion crowning the shaggy slopes of the highest hill in sight. Or as you slog up the winding track from Jericho and glimpse three towers stark against the sky, the desert sweeping up to its very skirts. Its heart-stopping quality springs from the fact that its reality so perfectly fits the mental images that have floated in the mind from a Bible-reading childhood.

Jerusalem ... Zion ... City of God ... City of Peace ... Eternal City ... City of David ... Mountain of the Lord ... Jerusalem the golden, with milk and honey blest ... Lift up your heads, O ye gates, and be ye lifted up ye everlasting doors ... I was glad when they said, Let us go up to the house of the Lord... *What is it about this place*? It has no mineral wealth, supports no industry, boasts no harbour, and stands on no river. Its agriculture is subsistence level, its water supply totally inadequate, and it sits astride no trade-route. Yet men have fought for it, women wept over it, armies clashed and collided around it. Oaths have been sworn by it, year-long pilgrimages undertaken to reach it, brutal crusades launched to capture it. Jews worldwide mark their calen-

dars with events that took place here. Muslims worldwide
are eager to engage in holy wars here. Christians worldwide trace their salvation and hope of heaven to what happened just outside these walls. The adherents of the only
three religions in the world that believe in one God also
believe that the last judgment will take place just east of
these ramparts. Modern American premillenialists look for
world cataclysm around these borders. Christians of all nations in their tens of millions encapsulate their hopes of a
new order and a new humanity in terms of a 'new Jerusalem
coming down out of heaven from God' (Rev. 21:9-11).

My first sight of it was from a taxi as we swung down the
road from Samaria. The driver seemed to have picked up
his American-English from a 1940s gangster film.

'Wadya make of this guy Josephus?' he asked without any
preliminaries, as we lurched into the mainstream traffic. 'Me,
I think he's just a traitor, but some reckon he was a patriot
and a great guy for puttin' history straight.'

He might have been referring to some contemporary politician. In fact he meant Joseph ben Matthias, who Romanised
his name to Flavius Josephus. He was born five years after
Jesus was crucified, and lived to the year 100. He led the
rebel forces in Galilee against the Romans, then changed
sides to become the Emperor's confidant and Middle East
war correspondent. But Jerusalem is like that. It is so im-
pregnated with its history that people live it, breathe it, argue and sing and write and fight about it. History, glorious
and tragic, truthful and mythical, is the Jerusalemite's ra-
tionale for every action, his alibi for every misdeed, his argument for being there at all.

Byzantines and all that

It is all a little confusing to the Christian tourist. The voluble guide waves a hand in the direction of yet another dusty pile of stones and says 'the remains of a Byzantine Church'. The tourist, punch-drunk with undigested facts, wonders whether a Byzantine Church was anything like a Baptist Church. Before he can explore the subject further, he is told, to his surprise, that a Crusader Church was built on top of it (Why on top? Was it not high enough?). He may even be told, with increasing bewilderment, that, of course, there was a Constantinian Church underneath it!

Of course, Constantinian, Byzantine and Crusader are not denominational titles like Methodist, Greek Catholic, Episcopalian. Rather they are descriptive of epochs and eras. On the lips of our loquacious guide they refer to historical periods (like Bronze Age or Elizabethan) and architectural designs (like Renaissance or Gothic). People didn't go around saying 'I'm a Byzantine Christian' or 'I attend a Constantinian Church' any more than people went around describing themselves as Bronze Age Nomads or Gothic Catholics. A church building is Constantinian if it was put up shortly after the Emperor Constantine declared himself and his empire Christian. Byzantine churches went up all over the place when the capital of that same crumbling empire was moved from Rome to Byzantium (Constantinople). Crusader churches were erected after those most unholy of Christian warriors tore the Holy Land temporarily out of the hands of the Muslims, and built churches everywhere in honour of the Prince of Peace.

Depressing and unconvincing though the layers of slightly different stone look to the uninstructed, they nevertheless stand for something very moving. They represent faith in

Christ and love of his name, stubbornly surviving the vicis-
situdes of political power struggles, racial tensions and ecclesiastical quarrels. The men and women who prayed and
sang in these successive buildings perpetuated through the
generations a love for the name of Jesus, that is recognisable
across the chasms of nationality, culture and theology that
separate them from us.

The other holocaust

In some cases there is not even a time gap. In the Armenian
quarter you can step back fifteen hundred years and meet
Christians whose churches were already ancient in Jerusalem
when the Crusaders turned up to 'rescue' them. This unique
community had their own holocaust, almost thirty years before
the Jews had theirs. Armenia in 1916, was a little nation-
state sandwiched between Russia and Turkey. The Turks,
embroiled in the First World War, saw Armenians as a threat,
for complex national, cultural, political and religious
reasons. So they set about the extermination of a race. Close
to two million were murdered, either killed in popular
pogroms, executed by the authorities, or sent off on
impossible overland treks in conditions that guaranteed the
death of the elderly, the sick and the young. Their homeland
is now indistinguishably shared by Muslim Turkey and ex-
Communist Russia. Perhaps six million of them are scattered
as international refugees – but some of them came 'home'.

For Armenians had always had another spiritual home.
Their land was the first kingdom in the world to declare
itself Christian. Evangelised (it is said) by Thaddeus and
Bartholomew from the first apostolic band, it had its little
persecuted churches from the beginning of the Gentile mission. In the year 301, a convert in the royal family by the

name of Gregory was imprisoned and tortured by the king's orders, but subsequently cured that same king of a mysterious disease and saw the whole state from the monarch downwards declared Christian.

Ever since, the story has been one of successive waves of violence and conquest lapping over the land. Romans, Persians, Arabs, Mongols, Mamelukes – they came and burned and killed and ruled – and went away again. Each time the Armenian survivors came back from the mountains where they had hidden with their national identity and their Christian faith intact.

When the Turks began to implement their 'final solution' (24 April 1915 is remembered annually as the Day of Infamy) about twelve hundred of the victims fled to Jerusalem. It was no strange city to Armenians. A list, still preserved from the fifth century, names seventy of their churche and monasteries in and around Jerusalem. In the tenth and eleventh centuries a series of Armenian women married successive Crusader kings of Jerusalem and became their Christian queens. Now, as a world war dragged to an exhausted halt, as Communist Russia was born, as Britain promised national independence to the Arabs and a national homeland to the Jews, the Armenian Christians made one quarter of biblical Jerusalem their home. There they preserve the heritage of a vanished kingdom in the hearts and minds of succeeding generations.

City behind the walls

Armenia-in-Jerusalem has its own walls within the city walls. You have a feeling of intrusion, almost of sacrilege, if you pluck up enough courage to step under an archway or push open an ancient door. Within these walls are more walls

again, surrounding silent sunlit courtyards. Always just beyond the corner of your eye and near the limit of your hearing is a whispering world of scuttling activity. The priests
(so many of them) wear black pointed cowls that cover all
of the head and most of the face, giving a sinister impression
which is unjustified but hard to shake off. Religion, educa-
tion, social life and embryonic politics are so closely inter-
woven that they are different facets of the same rough-cut
stone. The impression is of one vast monastery, yet twelve
hundred people live here. Property never passes into private hands. Each family has its own perpetual leasing rights,
kept within the family name. Incidentally every truly Armenian family name ends with the letters ...ian.

The great deep-throated bell of St James Cathedral
boomed out its call to worship as Rita and I wandered the
courts and exchanged smiles, signals, and broken English
with the very occasional passer-by. Behind the shining gold
icons, the hanging censers and gorgeous chandeliers, the slow
sonorous chanting and the incense smoke that catches eye
and throat, is a long-held faith in Christ, expressed in ways
alien to the evangelical Christian. I have no need and no
right to measure its reality and depth. But as we dropped
into the evangelical coffee-shop on the edge of the Armenian Quarter where a Muslim Arab and a Jewish yeshivah
student had come that day, enquiring the way of salvation in
Jesus, we found among the workers an Armenian!

The ruins that rose again
We hurried past the Zion Gate as we had so often before,
pausing only to glance at the bullet holes and shell splinters
from two wars. A few steps out of the Armenian Quarter
took us into an astonishingly different world. The Jewish

Quarter basked in golden sunshine.

It is a mistake often made by Christians to imagine that Jews only came back in force to Jerusalem in 1967. Only for short periods have they ever been missing since David the shepherd-king captured it 3,000 years ago. They were briefly expelled in 587 BC but were back within a half-century as their prophets had said they would be. Again in AD 70 they were hounded out by the Romans, and the process was furthered in 125. Their exile lasted longer that time. Rome tried to erase their memory from the pages of history, renaming Judea 'Palestine' (after their ancient enemies the Philistines) and rebuilding ruined Jerusalem as Aeola Capitolina. From then onwards, Jews were never more than a few miles away, and slipped back within the walls whenever successive occupiers permitted them. Otherwise, Jews throughout the world had to be content to face towards the temple site when they prayed, to greet each other with the pious wish, 'Next year in Jerusalem', and to pray, 'May we behold the merciful return to Zion'.

Muslim Arabs were kinder to Jewish Jerusalem than Byzantine Christians had been, and infinitely kinder than Crusaders would prove to be. In 638 the city fell to the Muslims.

When the Caliph Omar visited Jerusalem he asked the Jews: 'Where would you wish to live in the city?' They answered: 'In the southern part.' Their intention was to be close to the temple and its gate, as well as the waters of Siloam for ritual bathing. The Emir granted this to them.[2]

The 'Jewish Quarter' thus came into existence. The contemporary Arab account agrees with the above-quoted Jewish story: 'The Jewish community once more flourished, and Jews were among those who guarded the walls of the Dome of the Rock.... Jews made the glass and wicks for the oil lamps in Jerusalem from the eighth century onwards'.[3]

Four centuries later the Crusaders treated Jerusalem Jews abominably, murdering thousands, but did not completely expel them. When the Crusaders pulled out, the Jews were back in bigger numbers than ever. In 1187 the Ramban Synagogue was built in the Jewish Quarter (a place of worship until the Jordanians destroyed it in 1948). When the Turks renewed their rule of the city in 1840 there were 5,000 Jews, 4,600 Muslims and 3,300 Christians within the walls. When British General Allenby captured the city from the Turks in 1917 there were 32,000 Jews (three times more numerous than Muslims, eight times more numerous than Christians). Each of these figures had trebled again by 1948 when Israel became a state. By then thousands of Jews, of course lived in the new sprawling suburbs of West Jerusalem, way outside the ancient walls, just as many Palestinians, both Christian and Muslim, lived in East Jerusalem, also outside the walls. For the next nineteen years Jewish houses in the Old City were wrecked, their graves desecrated, their synagogues reduced to rubble and their Quarter turned into a rubbish tip.

Whatever the rights and wrongs of the 1967 Six Day War, the Israelis can hardly be accused of coming as alien interlopers with their only argument proceeding from the barrel of a gun. They were coming home, at least in the Jewish Quarter. The first thing they had to do was rebuild it. The traditional style has been reproduced. Only one road permits traffic, along the edge of the Armenian and Jewish Quarters. The rest is all narrow arched lanes, gold-and-green sunlit squares, simple but elegant synagogues and flat-roofed houses. The old folk sit in the sun and talk; and the children play in the streets as the prophet said they would.

The wall that was built downwards

There are many wonders to delay the wanderer in the Jewish Quarter, but we were hurrying this day to a private house that epitomises them all. Number 7 Hagitit Street is the home of the Siebenbergs. We had first learned of them through a National Geographical video purchased at Woolworths in the north of England. At one o'clock most afternoons you can call on Theo and Miriam – and have a look at 3,000 years of history. Miriam is a 'sabra', born in Israel. Theo hails from Belgium where he made his money with diamonds before fleeing the Nazis. Having dug wealth from the earth (so to speak) he is now putting it back by the million to uncover a different kind of gem.

In 1970 the family fulfilled a life ambition and became residents of Jerusalem, purchasing one of the new-built houses in the Jewish Quarter. It stood on a hillock of earth, rock and debris. Seeing the famous Cardo Dig going on only 200 yards away, Theo asked the archaeologists what chance there was of anything significant lying under his house. 'No chance at all,' he was told. 'But that doesn't seem right to me,' he replied. 'The temple was just over there. Why wouldn't Jews have built here then?' 'It's just not on,' was their repeated answer.

He thought it over, talked it over, dreamed about it, until it became an obsession. So he approached architects and engineers. 'What would be the problems if I dug below my floors?' he asked.

They were uniformly horrified. Not only would his own half-million dollar house fall inwards, but the surrounding apartments and houses would slide sideways down the slope. But, continually pestered, the experts grudgingly accepted a theoretical possibility. At a price something like six times the cost of the house, it could be possible to build a retaining wall downwards from the surface, held in place by dozens of steel anchors. That was enough. With the help of friends, volunteers, paid workers and a line of donkeys, the Siebenbergs began an eight-year task. For two years they found nothing significant. Then there came to light a bronze ring-shaped key. The Talmud discusses the thing, and the problem it raises. Can a good Jew wear it on the Sabbath, since it can be regarded as a tool? Their conclusion was – if bronze, no, for it is indeed a tool. If silver, yes, for now it is clearly an ornament; you don't make tools out of silver. A piece of Jewish life and tradition, frozen in time.

Now the discoveries came tumbling out. A cistern was dated by a certain-shaped cross on the plaster, until some of the plaster was removed, and revealed stone walls built a hundred years before Christ. Soon its fate became poignantly evident. Layers of black compressed carbon marked its destruction in AD 70, as the triumphant Romans swept into the Upper City, a month after sacking the Temple. Josephus fixes the day for us: 8th Elum. A seal of the Tenth Legion confirms that this was indeed, as the records say, the notorious legion that accomplished the grim task. Horrible nails, long, thick blunt-headed, only partly rusted, speak grimly of the fate of crucifixion that awaited many terrified inhabitants.

They dug deeper – and struck the line of the famous water-channel by which Herod piped supplies from 'Solomon's Pools' near Bethlehem, seventeen miles in a straight line, but forty miles by the route it had to follow, pursuing the contours, occasionally crossing a ravine by aqueduct, slowly, slowly descending at an incline of one in a thousand, until at last it reached the Temple. Supplies of water for a quarter of a million animal sacrifices at the great festivals flowed through this brilliant feat of engineering and through the Siebenbergs' basement.

They dug further and found a glass horn with animal-head decorations, almost unique. There are five others known in the world and all are linked with King Mombas, son of Queen Helene of Abilene, who converted with all of her African tribe to Judaism. She was buried north of the city, near the Garden Tomb. He, according to tradition, lived in the Upper City within sight of the Temple. In fact, in the Siebenbergs' cellar, it seems.

They dug again. Three storeys down is 800 BC, Isaiah's time. The northern kingdom of Israel had fallen to the Assyrians, but good king Hezekiah of Judah held out, urged by the prophet to trust in God. Many northern refugees fled to Jerusalem, and for the first time the western hill became a city suburb. It lasted until Jeremiah's time. Then, as that weeping preacher had warned, the terrible Babylonians succeeded where the Assyrians had failed. The Siebenbergs found arrowheads and spearheads from the battle: Rita and I stared at them with awe, and imagined we could hear the clash and shout of fighting.

With superb irony, on the same day that some of the arrowheads were found, a rusty but recognisable Czech submachine gun was unearthed, dated 1948. We know who its owner was. The Jews only had two such guns to defend themselves against the onslaught of well equipped Jordanian soldiers. The two owners ran and weaved and dodged and ducked, firing from different positions to give the impression that they were many. Eventually Riz of Mizaki was killed, and the next day the Quarter was evacuated. Sorrowing colleagues threw his gun down a disused cistern – into the

Siebenbergs' historical hole-in-the-ground.

So the discoveries went on. Now the dig is complete, Theo and Miriam have installed an exhibition and a slide presentation. They have plans to turn that vast cistern into a musical auditorium. For they found in it an ancient musical instrument, a bronze music-bell. When a choir of young Israelis visited the excavation and stood awed at the bottom of the cistern, they spontaneously began to sing in haunting five-point harmony the psalm, 'Out of the depths I cry unto you, Lord.'

We climbed back up to ground level, and talked in the sunshine at the front door. I spoke of including our visit in the book I was writing.

'What is it about?'

'Well – a kind of theological walkabout. I thought of calling it *A Preacher Walks Through the Promised Land*.'

Eyes twinkled. 'I thought someone had done that already – about 1,900 years ago!'

He showed me a note in the visitors' book from a fellow Belgian Jew. 'To have saved one soul is to have redeemed the world. To have built one house and revealed all that lies beneath it is to have resurrected our people's tower to the heavens.'

Mosques and Minarets

Take a few steps out of the Jewish into the Arab Quarter and the contrast is dramatic. It is more colourful, more noisy, more crowded, more dirty. The sounds and smells are totally different. The (to us) alien chant, part moan, part yell, part gargle echoes hauntingly from a dozen minarets. Tiny shops, six foot square cubes in crumbling walls, offer their wares as shopkeepers shout and gesticulate and haggle. They look like Ali Baba's forty thieves, but they have a code of honour all their own. Tourists are charged double the expected price and have to reduce it with prolonged argument and counter-offer. Local residents get the goods cheaper; you only have to be introduced once and are then instantly recognised. 'Reedah – you buy theeze,' called out one cheeky proprietor to Rita as she passed the second time. Arabs get a further reduction, and relatives a further reduction again.

The lanes and alleys are narrow, arched, winding and crowded. Jostling throngs of every conceivable nationality push and heave and scramble. Americans with dark glasses and video machines, Germans with grotesque nose-shields and cameras, pale-faced English with multicoloured flight-bags, Finns and Italians, Ghanians and Kenyans, Japanese and Philippinos, West Indians and Latin-Americans, many wearing exotic national dress as if to underline that their people have really come *here*. Arab head-dresses splash the heaving crowds with black and white or red check, and about one in every fifteen looks uncomfortably like Yasser Arafat. Arab women sport embroidered dresses that tell you, if you have the clue, which village they hail from. Bedouin embroidery in cubes and whorls relates the family history in symbols: births, marriages and deaths for a couple of centuries back. Some of the women crouch on any available step, a handful of herbs or a basketful of fruit for sale.

And there are priests and clerics everywhere. Varieties of Christianity unknown to British Protestants bid for attention in the exotic diversity of colour and shape of their head-dresses. Jews seem quite at home, too. Sweeping self-consciously down the short-cut to the Wall, they flaunt their swashbuckling prayer-shawls, huge bobbing fur hats proclaim Russia as the country of origin for some, and multi-

coloured turbans topping white robes proclaim Ethiopia as
the home of others. What exactly *is* a Jew, one wonders again,
when he can be black African, brown Yemeni, black-bearded
Polish or red-faced American?

Golden dome and silver sanctuary

The glory of the Arab Quarter is the gigantic Dome of the
Rock, called the Mosque of Omar. It is an enormous shrine,
not for corporate acts of worship but for individual visitors
of any race and creed (as long as you remove your shoes and
it isn't Friday).

Its dimensions are awesome, its golden dome magnificent, its myriad multi-coloured mosaics breathtaking. For
centuries Jewish tradition identified the rock that now thrusts
through its floor as the summit of the mountain of Moriah,
where Abraham almost sacrificed Isaac. Here Solomon's
temple later stood. In Crusader times there was a great Christian shrine hereabouts. When the world was thought to be a
flat disc, this area was considered the centre.

When Caliph Omar conquered the city in 638, he did erect
a mosque, but this was not it; this is a shrine, not a mosque.
The silver-topped Aksa mosque was built nearby, on the
same flat platform of rock originally laid by Herod's work-
men. It is the third most holy site of Islam, after Mecca and
Medina. Respectful though Muslims were of Abraham and
Isaac, something a little more Islamic was felt to be necessary. So Ishmael the Arab neatly replaced Isaac the Jew in
the biblical story. And for good measure it was suggested
that Mohammed, who undoubtedly visited the city, here
mounted a magical horse at this spot and thence rode to
heaven. The mark left by the sole of his feet will be shown
to you on request.

The entire Temple Mount platform is called Haram el-Shariff (the Noble Sanctuary). Its atmosphere is palpable, unique, slightly frightening. Devout Jews refuse to put a foot in the whole area, for fear of inadvertently treading where the Holy of Holies once stood, forbidden to any but the High Priest once a year. It is by no means certain that the floor of the Dome marks the exact spot. Complicated calculations recently carried out suggest that a point 150 yards north of the Dome is the right place. The tiny Dome of the Tablets is in direct line with the Golden Gate, the ancient entry which stood directly opposite the Altar of Burnt Offering and the door of the Sanctuary. This suggestion had caused a good deal of embarrassment to the Arabs and a quiver of excitement to those Jews and Christians whose prophetic scenario includes a rebuilding of the Temple. Walk anywhere near the Dome of the Tablets nowadays and you will get suspicious looks and a curt wave of dismissal from the Waqf (Islamic guards). Display a camera or a tape-measure and you are likely to get run off. I managed a quick snap by standing with my back to it and employing some deft and surreptitious gymnastics.

On Fridays the whole area is one mass of multicoloured head-dresses and trouser suits as uncountable thousands pour up the steps and through the arches to stand, kneel and prostrate themselves in prayer. On other days visitors are cautiously welcome if they keep the rules. Reveal bare arms or legs and you will be forcibly enveloped in a pale blue piece of shapeless material smelling of goodness knows what and stained with sweat. Men and women must not hold hands here. A young couple near me were curtly told to stop. Having no idea of the language they nervously clung to each other all the more, only to be violently harangued. A whispered

explanation defused the situation, and the guard marched off
with a snarl.

The atmosphere is often tense. Christian tourists want to
see it, yet shrink from it. Some of them seriously regard the
Dome as 'the abomination that causes desolation, standing
in the holy place' (Dan. 11:31 and Matt. 24:15). I understand their concern, but question their theology and their history.

Arab feeling soon runs high here, and is expressed in anti-
Christian and anti-Jewish frenzy. Mullahs shouting over the
minarets' loud-speakers can turn a congregation into a ram-
paging mob within minutes. As I write, I have watched on
the TV screen Israeli soldiers dispersing one such mob with
tear-gas and four-foot truncheons whilst snipers deploy
around the walls. In 1969 the mosque was mysteriously
arsonised, and Arabs will earnestly assure you that the Jerusalem fire service took two hours to respond. A demented
Australian Christian tossed hand-grenades to speed the
Dome's demolition and hasten the rebuilding of the Temple.
An American-Israeli soldier went out of his mind and opened
fire on worshippers with a machine-gun. A Jewish terrorist
group were caught trying to dynamite the mosque (with magnificent impartiality their colleagues planted hand-grenades
in Muslim prayer-rooms and Catholic churches, and set the
Baptist Chapel in West Jerusalem on fire). At the end of
1996 the world watched as bloody fighting raged here over
the opening of a Jewish tunnel which was felt to threaten the
mosque. Religion, politics and racialism form a heady and
dangerous mix in the Noble Sanctuary.

Christian Quarter

Our imaginary walk, recalling many a literal walk of my
own, has taken us anti-clockwise from a starting point at the
Jaffa Gate (nine o'clock, so to speak). The final quarter is
thus the 'Christian' area, roughly between twelve and three.
This too is Arabic, but in a strikingly different way. For of
course many Arabs are Christians, usually Roman Catholic
or Orthodox. This north-west section houses many churches,
convents and monasteries. The main road (pedestrian only)
is called Eastern Patriarchate Street. Most of the shops sell
religious souvenirs. The boom, clang and tinkle of church
bells can be heard everywhere. Somewhere in this area, but
outside the walls of Jesus' time, the crucifixion took place.
That requires a later chapter to itself.

References
1. Talmud, *Kiddushim*, 49b.
2. Sefer Ha Yishuv, 'Getting Jerusalem Together' (Fran Albert,
Archaeological Seminar Ltd, 1984), p. 32.
3. Mujir al-Din, 'History of Jerusalem and Hebron', Quoted from *Getting Jerusalem Together*, p. 33.

6

For Zion's Sake

Simcha Dimitz was for some years Israel's Ambassador in Washington. He liked to tell of a lecture he once gave in an American black church. 'After my talk, a young girl came up to me and said, "Where do you live?" I said, "Jerusalem." She thought about that for a minute and said, "Jerusalem, is that a place on earth? I thought it was in heaven." That's when I really understood that Jerusalem symbolizes every wish, every hope, every dream, every ideal. Everyone sees it how they want to see it. It may be the capital of Israel, but in every heart is a little bit of Jerusalem.'[1]

Jews have always understood that; hence the haunting, wistful centuries-long greeting, 'Next year in Jerusalem'. For most of them there was not the slightest prospect of a literal fulfilment, and yet Zion, City of God, House of the Lord, City of David were deep chords that struck to the very heart of what it meant to be a Jew; indeed of what it meant to believe in the Living God.

The Christian feels it too. On my first walk through the city I had an almost mystic sense that I knew the place well – had *always* known it. Perhaps a tribute to the accuracy of children's illustrated Bibles? More than that, I think! For I was walking in the Jerusalem of Jesus, and he has been the towering figure in my life for fifty-five years. In these streets he healed the lame and the blind. Among those colonnades he taught the word of life. Outside those walls he died for my salvation.

To spend a month at the Hebrew University studying their

course, 'Jerusalem Through The Ages' was one of the most fascinating and unforgettable experiences of my life. That was before I went to live there, and my only previous knowledge was based on one private trip and two 'Christian Tours'. Now the whole thing came together, as with meticulous scholarship and careful understatement archaeologists led us forward through every era from David's coup a thousand years before Christ, to General Allenby's ejection of the Turks during the First World War.

Most of the lectures were 'on site'. We explored the tunnel through which David sent his commandos, and fingered the quarried stone with which Solomon built the Temple. We stared in awe at the 'broad wall' just rediscovered, which anxious king Hezekiah extended to keep out the threatening Babylonian army.

We debated the likely location of Pilate's fortress in the time of Jesus, and met the man who had found the stone inscription in Caesarea which provided first independent evidence of Pontius Pilate's procuratorship.

We watched the preliminary digging that would later uncover and then restore the Roman Cardo Maxima, the main shopping street built after AD 150. We discussed how reliable or otherwise was Helena's hunt for Christian holy sites, when the emperor became a Christian. We speculated on the location of Justinian's great Byzantine church. We learned of the logic behind Islam's seizure of the city, and were shown how to recognize the invariable marks of that culture: the domed roof, the warren of interconnected family homes, the public fountain, the school and the mosque. We followed the desperate attempts by Crusaders to reconquer the city and smiled at their often ham-fisted attempts to identify sites associated with Jesus.

Much of this can now be seen in the course of any well-organised pilgrimage-holiday to the Holy Land, as long as the viewer is willing to do without much sleep for ten days!

The Israeli Ambassador was quite right; Jerusalem has come to mean very varied things to many different people; a symbol either emerging from the depths of the human psyche ... or planted there by God ... or both ?

Jebusite Fortress

To David it was the new capital for the rather loosely united tribes. Brilliant strategist that he was, he chose a town with no earlier Israelite history that could be claimed by one exclusive element or tribe. In fact it had to be conquered and occupied as the first step. Then he brought the sacred Ark of the Covenant to its new centre, thus combining wilderness worship with the new settled religious cult (2 Sam. 6).

The ancient Jebusite fortress thus upgraded to House of God actually stood outside and to the south-east of the present city walls, nestled on the Ophel ridge, a long hump of stony ground that slopes down below what was to become the Temple Mount. Walk down the Kidron Valley, with the ridge on your right. You will be met by numerous touters of archaeological finds real and bogus, at least half of whom will assure you that they once personally worked for Dame Katherine Kenyon! Here is the Gihon Spring, main source of water for the ancient city.

Scramble into the cave and follow the flow of water (unless there has been recent rain. Before it bends and becomes Hezekiah's tunnel (of which more anon) it opens up above your head as a natural 'chimney'. This was the secret access which enabled the defenders to hide the spring from their besiegers whilst tapping its supply themselves.

Secure on the ramparts above, they taunted David, claiming that their invalids could defend the fortress single-handed. David's response was to send his SAS up the crazy climb. They broke out into the street above, and won the day. The odd little story is recorded in 2 Samuel 5:6-8 and 1 Chronicles 11:4-9. David's advice, 'you will have to use the water-shaft' carried little meaning to readers until a couple of Victorian characters rediscovered the scene of the exploit. Captain Charles Warren of the British army, a Richard Hannay kind of figure, was aided by his indefatigable adjutant, Corporal Birtles. They arrived in Jerusalem in 1867 with a commission from the Palestine Exploration Fund to reconstruct on paper the topography of the ancient city, buried as it now was under a literal mountain of rubbish and a metaphorical mountain of Turkish mistrust and bureaucracy. In a remarkable feat of mountaineering, they struggled upwards through black tunnels, caves and fissures, and emerged, as David's commandos had done, in the city a hundred feet above.

Nowadays it is all so easy; you can walk to their point of emergence, view an explanatory exhibition, edge down a few yards of wooden walkway, peer down the hole, and use your imagination.

To the ancient psalmists the fortress of Zion, soon to have a temple to house the Ark, was both symbol and concrete expression of the presence of God with his people, the successor to Sinai as sign of God's covenant. It is spelled out explicitly in Psalm 68, especially verses 8 and 17, but constantly hinted at in numerous songs and prayers.

God's Statesman

Two centuries after Solomon, in the time of the prophet Isaiah, city and temple alike stood as symbols of God's faithfulness. The city now extended north and west, covering perhaps three-quarters of a square mile. The dreaded Assyrians, after swallowing nation after nation in their relentless conquests, had reached Jerusalem with a besieging army. Devout king Hezekiah was influenced and supported by the prophet. In one of the Bible's most famous and dramatic scenes, the king cries to God in penitence and faith. The encircling army melts away in mysterious circumstances that find an echo in both Assyrian and Egyptian accounts (2 Kgs. 18-19; Isa. 36-37).

> The divine promise stood:
> Like birds hovering overhead the Lord Almighty
> will shield Jerusalem and deliver it (31:5).
>
> I will defend this city and save it
> for my sake and the sake of David my servant (37:35).

Highly symbolic terms express God's purpose; the wolf at peace with the lamb, swords turned into farming tools, David's throne established forever, a mountain-top banquet for all nations. Clearly more is in view than the physical survival of a tiny city-state at a particular moment in time. Yet it was indeed a particular moment, and a particular physical threat was averted. So do the spiritual and the secular, the symbolic and the literal, the temporal and eternal coalesce in this unique city.

Their defensive works have been uncovered in the last decade. A section of what is now called 'the Broad Wall' was unearthed during restoration work near the Roman

Cardo, and now stands exposed, as thick as the width of a country road. You peer 14 feet down from the present street level and wonder at the sight; a 130-foot length of wall 27 centuries old, 23 feet wide and about 30 feet high. At two points its line cuts through the remains of older houses, exactly as the prophet described: 'You tore down houses to strengthen the wall' (Isa. 22:10). The archaeologist in charge, revered Nahman Avigad, saw at once the implications. Only a king could have ordered such a wall, demolishing almost-new houses in the process. Only a major crisis could have justified it. Hezekiah's story exactly fitted the situation.

The biblical chronicler, probably writing 200 years later, tells us that 'Hezekiah worked hard repairing all the broken sections of the wall and building towers on it. He built another wall outside that one and reinforced the supporting terraces of the city of David' (2 Chr. 32:5).

Hezekiah's Tunnel

Captain Warren and his adjutant come to our aid once more, as we try to imagine the feeling of those dramatic days. Having solved the secret of the vertical tunnel (henceforth christened Warren's Shaft) they continued to explore the horizontal tunnel. Wading for almost a mile, water up to their waists and the rock sides scraping their shoulders and heads, they emerged an hour later at the far side of the ridge, into what was already known to be the Pool of Siloam, the scene of one of Jesus' miracles (John 9). They had discovered 'Hezekiah's Tunnel', and with it the meaning of another two enigmatic Bible references.

Hezekiah made the pool and the tunnel by which he brought water into the city (2 Kgs. 20:20).

He consulted with his officials and military staff about blocking
off the water from the springs outside the city, and they helped him
(2 Chron. 32:1-4).

Twelve years later Arab children playing in the tunnel (the
water level falls in the dry season) found an ancient inscription marking the point where Hezekiah's diggers, working
from both ends at once, met in the middle. It must have been
a dramatic moment, and their technology still puzzles us.
The inscription does justice to the event: 'Axe to axe they
cut, each man towards his fellow. Whilst there were yet three
cubits to be cut through, the voice of one man calling to the
other was heard. When the tunnel was driven through, the
excavators met man to man, pick to pick, the water flowed
for 1,200 cubits from the spring to the reservoir.'[3]

The 'spring' was of course the Gihon Spring, from which
Warren's shaft led. The 'reservoir' was the Pool of Siloam,
which means 'Sent'. The nickname highlighted the way the
water was so ingeniously sent through the rocky ridge. John,
in his account of Jesus' healing of the blind man, in a manner
typical of him, suggests a further symbolic meaning, as the
man is sent by Jesus to wash and be whole.

A controversial dig

Religious dispute continued to plague the resumption of the
archaeological search for the relationship between David's
city and Isaiah's Jerusalem. The City of David Society was
formed, and Dr Yigal Shiloh gathered professionals and volunteers from all over the world. Orthodox Jews in their black
frock coats and homburg hats stoned the excavators, leaped
into the newly dug trenches, prostrated themselves over the
discoveries, struggled with the police, and surrounded the
dig with chanting banner carriers. Their objections were

largely based on the pious Jewish revulsion against disturbing the buried dead of recent or long past generations.

On-site lectures were impossible. A few of us crawled on our tummies up to the barbed wire, and hazarded guesses about the identity of a strange structure slowly being uncovered. Shaped like a giant bee-hive, built of overlapping stones, its unearthing made the newspaper headlines for weeks. Was it the true tomb of King David? Did the slightly pyramidal shape suggest a monument to Solomon's Egyptian princess? Was it a vault guarding temple treasure?

The truth, it is now believed, is only slightly less dramatic than the speculation. The structure proved to be solid. It seems to be a surviving buttress of a retaining wall on which the Jebusite fortress perched half-way up the slope. Its solid bulk suggests that it supported a tower or a gatehouse. This could well be what in turn became David's citadel. In the most basic sense of that many-layered word, it seems that Zion has been discovered.

Eight years of digging, sifting, clearing and reconstructing followed. The excavation is now complete, with part of the area laid out as an archaeological garden with walkways and explanatory plaques. Beside the citadel wall are houses that were part-destroyed in the tragic climax of 586 BC, when the Babylonians were divinely permitted to achieve what the Assyrians were forbidden. Jerusalem was overrun, as the weeping prophet Jeremiah had warned would happen.

Arrow-heads bear silent witness to the fighting. Charred beams and furniture portray its outcome. 'The commander of the imperial guard of Nebuchadnezzar came to Jerusalem .... every important building he burned down .... and carried into exile the people that remained' (2 Kgs. 25:8-11).

In one of the houses an intriguing discovery was made. A *Bulla* is a kind of signet ring shaped in stone, with which an autograph or personal mark was pressed onto the wax seal of a closed 'book' or scroll. Jeremiah 32:9-15 gives an example of its use. In what was clearly an administrative office near the citadel, fifty Bullae were found. Each bears an inscription, 'belonging to...' and a personal name. Three of them are names that appear in a poignant biblical episode set at this very time.

The prophet Jeremiah dictates to his secretary (scribe) Baruch warnings of divine judgement, to be read aloud to the king. The brave yet nervous officials arrange the public reading, and the scene is set as the ruler sits in his winter apartment, with a fire burning in the brazier in front of him. Furious at what he hears, he slashes the scroll to pieces with a knife, and throws the fragments on the fire. Then he sends an order for the arrest of the prophet and the scribe: 'The king commanded Jerahmeal, a son of the king, Seraiah son of Azriel and Shelemiah son of Abdeel to arrest Baruch the scribe and Jeremiah the prophet. But the LORD had hidden them' (Jer. 36:26).

The names on the recovered Bullae include 'Jerahmeel the king's son', 'Seraiahu' and 'Berachiah (Baruch), son of the scribe'.

Under the temple shadow

Of course the structure that dominates all these events is the temple. The presence of God, symbolised in the worship centred there, was the groundstone of that 'invioability of Zion', as the theologians call it, which Isaiah proclaimed yet Jeremiah a century later denied. In that paradoxical fact lies a timely warning not to pin all our beliefs about Jerusalem (ancient or modern) to a few selected texts, to the ignoring of others. Jerusalem is secure because God is faithful, said Isaiah (31:4-5). Jerusalem will perish because Israel has broken covenant, said Jeremiah, yet the city will live again (Jer. 21:3-7; 33:9). There is no permanent city for us here on earth, says a later Hebrew writer – but you have come to Jerusalem when you have come to Jesus (Heb. 13:14; 12:22-24). All three statements are words from God. It is indeed a complex task to 'unpack the layers of meaning behind the incredible concept of that city', as Adrian Snell attempts to do in his musical, *City of Peace*.

The original temple was built by Solomon's workers and repaired after destruction under Ezra's direction. In Jesus' time immense rebuilding, enlarging and beautifying took place at Herod's orders, and the result is usually called the Second Temple. The excavation of this site has become the glory of modern Israel's archaeological endeavour, the crown and climax of their research. Any Christian visiting the city should insist on a full day of guided tour of the excavations. The purchase of one of the available illustrated guidebooks of this area will surpass the value of all your other tourist purchases put together.

The subject is intensely emotional. The very mention of Professor Meir Ben-Dov can ruin a mayor's cocktail party or a scientific seminar. Breaking all of the accepted rules and introducing techniques that scandalised the scientific world, Ben-Dov laboured for twelve years, twelve months per year.

They could only excavate near the Temple Mount, since political and religious pressure from Jew and Arab alike forbad any intrusion onto the platform itself. As it was, for many successive years the United Nations passed a stern forbidding order on any research in the area whatever; a resolution that was cheerfully ignored as regularly as it was proposed. The whole area of the Noble Sanctuary (to give its Islamic name) was out of bounds, but fortunately the temple of Jesus' time, vastly rebuilt by Herod the Great, covered an even greater area. Around it stood a huge complex of porticoes, courts, esplanades, staircases, ritual baths and ancillary buildings, encompassing one and a half million square feet. Some of this was *outside* the colossal retaining walls built by Herod to support the area; walls 165 feet high, of which the *Kotel* (the famous Western or Wailing Wall) is a partial survivor.

The normal tools of an archaeologist are a hand trowel and a camel hair handbrush. Ben-Dov brought in a bulldozer. Horizontally he cut great swathes with this machine, whilst vertically he sunk shafts so as to anticipate the strata that the machine would expose. 'If the bulldozer operator is graced with a sensitive soul, and if an archaeologist is stationed permanently beside the scoop, it can be a very helpful instrument,' he explained blandly.

Benjamin Mazor, the overall Director, eventually fell out with his Field Director Ben-Dov, and they produced what amounted to rival preliminary reports, or rather popular and extremely readable books.[3]

The most dramatic find was the Southern Staircase, sometimes called the Rabbis' Steps. Each 200 feet long, the great white steps provided the main entry to the sanctuary for the local populace, who in Jesus' time still lived in the now poor quarter of the old city of David. Alternating steps are twelve and thirty-five inches broad, to prevent too-hurried entrance of the thousands who streamed in. They would have taken two hours to enter during the major festivals. The human streams then narrowed through a double and a treble gate, which led to upward sloping tunnels that eventually emerged through the flow of the temple courts themselves (what Josephus calls the Outer Court, and the New Testament the Court of the Gentiles).

Josephus describes the brightly painted decorations on the walls and ceiling of the tunnel, and faded evidence of this was found in broken fragments that have fallen out and therefore became available to the diggers. To my dismay the paintings have led some scholars to conclude that this is what the New Testament calls the Beautiful Gate, at which the apostles healed a lame man (Acts 3:1-10), whereas the location was previously thought to be on the inner side of the Eastern (Golden) Gate which leads to Solomon's Portico, where the early church met. However, three days before I re-wrote this paragraph, Dr. Dan Bahat, Chief Archaeologist for Jerusalem, whilst visiting London, assured me that in his opinion my preferred option was still his choice. 'For once, the Crusaders got it right; a circumstance so unlikely that it tends to bias scholars against that choice,' he commented cheerfully.

Soon after the Staircase was discovered, the Patriarch of the ancient Ethiopian Church visited the dig. He asked, 'Is it possible that Jesus and his Apostles walked up these steps?' Ben-Dov assured him that there was no doubt of it. A wave of emotion swept over the churchman and his retinue, and they paused to offer prayers on the spot. It is now virtually certain that Jesus not only walked here, but taught here. For this is where the Pharisees, that is the laymen who taught the Scriptures, often stood to harangue and debate with the slow-moving queues of pilgrims and worshippers: hence the nickname of the Rabbis' Staircase. The Sadducees, on the other hand, were the 'clergy', who served in the inmost-but-one Court of the Priests.

Jesus had other preaching venues, actually inside the temple enclosure. John's Gospel, uniquely, tells of frequent visits to the shrine during the various annual festivals.[4] In winter Jesus used for his preaching the partial shelter of Solomon's Colonnade, on the eastern side of the court (John 10:22-23). This was regarded as the most holy because the steep fall of the valley made it impossible for Herod to enlarge the platform in that direction, so the feeling was that this ground was doubly holy, going back as it did to earlier and better days. Here the early church met for worship and teaching (Acts 3:11; 5:12).

English farmer, Alec Garrard[5], whose remarkable and meticulously researched model of the temple stands in his Suffolk barn, tells me that Jesus must also have been invited to preach much 'further in' to the temple courts, with its carefully graded areas, for he sat and commented, and even gave formal teaching discourses, as the people put their money in 'the Treasury', which was situated very close to the Holiest Place.[6] The teacher sat to speak, whilst the hearers stood to listen.

Another striking find at the foot of the Staircase was the series of mikvaot, stepped baths where Jews performed the required ritual ablutions, and Gentile converts were immersed. Modern Baptists are always delighted to see them. There are at least thirty baths, and here is a possible venue for the mass-baptisms by immersion that followed Peter's preaching on the Day of Pentecost (Acts 2: 38-41). At the very least, their discovery explodes the often-expressed objection that 3,000 baptisms by any method other than sprinkling were impossible!

Although the original 12-year excavations are long-since over, another phase was begun in 1995, and continues to this day. The finds are less dramatic, but significant and controversial. The actual pavement from Jesus' time has been unearthed, just south of the Wailing Wall. A row of shops, partly underneath the remains of a great ornamental royal staircase, probably include the booths of the money-changers who, with the sellers of sacrificial animals, aroused the anger of Jesus.

The most controversial development has been the enlargement of a tunnel northward alongside the continuation of the Western Wall. The creation of a second entry and exit in the Via Dolorosa caused a bloody explosion of political and religious conflict for a week in December 1996, and the 'Peace Process' seemed for a time to be in ruins. Absurdly, it was dubbed by the media the Aska Mosque Tunnel, and certainly thousands of Palestinians became convinced that its purpose was to undermine their sacred site. In actual fact it began a good quarter mile from the mosque, ran *away* from it *outside* the temple area, at an ever diverging angle.

In fact its main line has been known for a hundred years, and some of its length was explored fifteen years ago. A rather furtive visit was organised for students of the 'Jerusalem Through The Ages' course. We explored in some awe, accompanied by soldiers nervously fingering their guns. It is a combination of natural rock faults, artificially dug tunnels, and ancient cisterns and water channels, all running parallel with the outside of the Western Wall. It enables scholars to establish with a high degree of certainty the site of the original Holy of Holies (not, of course in the tunnel, but many yards to the east, and very much higher).

The hair on my neck prickled as I examined the exits of

channels that had carried away blood and water in immense quantities from the sacrifices and lustrations of almost a thousand years, from Solomon's time to that of Jesus. Since then an almost unbelievably large stone in Herod's temple wall has been uncovered, weighing an estimated 500 tons. Warren's Gate has been rediscovered; the entrance found by the Victorian Sir Charles Warren who risked his life sinking deep vertical shafts, from which he then burrowed sideways and vertically, to get around Turkish restrictions. This in turn establishes the line of the 'middle wall of partition' as Paul calls it (Eph. 2:14 AV, the dividing wall of hostility, RSV).

This barrier between the outer 'Court of the Gentiles' and the rest of the area, was forbidden on pain of death to any non-Jews. Josephus describes it, and fragments of the warning notices have already been found. Paul was almost lynched because of a false rumour that he smuggled Gentile Christians beyond this point (Acts 21:27-32). The tunnel has aroused modern Jewish anger as well as Arab feeling. By establishing the line of forbidden entry, the archaeologists have unavoidably implied that the section of the Wailing Wall held sacred for two thousand years actually bordered the area in which 'unclean' Gentiles were allowed. Some of the most strictly orthodox Jews have therefore simply denied the whole discovery and its implications!

Rich in symbolism, the ruined and restored city continues to signal different messages to different people. Truly, as the black girl reminded the ambassador, everyone sees the city as they want to see it. Christian hymnology certainly supports that idea. We sing of Jerusalem the golden, with milk and honey blest (or at least we did before the advent of the overhead projector!). We encouraged each other as we marched upward to Zion, the beautiful city of God (we meant heaven). Yet other hymns placed it firmly on earth, as the people of God, the Church. 'City of God, how broad and far outstretch thy walls sublime .... one holy church, one army strong' we sang. And 'Glorious things of thee are spoken, Zion city of our God'. Yes, and even when we discard our hymnbooks and switch on the projector, we celebrate 'Mount Zion on the side of the north, the city of the great king' (Psalm 48) and then switch to 'One Lord, one faith, one body' (Eph 4). Always assuming that we know what we are singing, we thus bear witness to the one symbolised and fulfilled in the other.

References

1. Quoted from D J Wiseman, 'Siloam' in *The New Bible Dictionary*, IVP, 1961, p. 1187.
2. See *Jerusalem Past and Present in the Purposes of God*, ed PWL Walker, Tyndale House, Cambridge, 1992, especially 'Jerusalem in the Old Testament' by Gordon McConville within that volume.
3. Meir Ben-Dov, *In the Shadow of the Temple*, Harper and Row, New York, 1985. Benjamin Mazor, *Mountain of the Lord*, Doubleday, New York, 1975 (with Gaalyah Cornfeld and David Noel Freedman).
4. Donald Bridge, *Why Four Gospels?*, Mentor, 1996, Chapter 15.
5. Suffolk Farm temple model: Alec Garrard, Moat Farm, Fressingfield, Eye, Suffolk. Viewing only possible by prior arrangement, telephone 01379 86 308.
6. Mark 12:41-43; John 8:20.

Part Three

The Teacher

About that time there lived Jesus, a wise man, if indeed
one ought to call him a man. For he was one who wrought
surprising feats and was a teacher of such people as accept
the truth gladly.... And the tribe of the Christians so called
after him, has still to this day not disappeared
(Flavius Josephus – around 90 AD).

Jesus! the name that charms our fears,
That bids our sorrows cease;
'Tis music in the sinner's ears,
'Tis life, and health, and peace.
(Charles Wesley – around 1745)

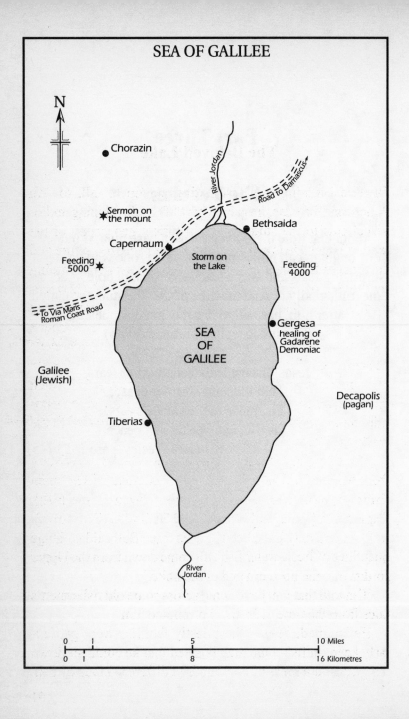

SEA OF GALILEE

N

Chorazin

Sermon on
the mount

River Jordan

Road to Damascus

Bethsaida

Capernaum

Storm on
the Lake

Feeding
5000

Feeding
4000

To Via Maris
Roman Coast Road

Gergesa
healing of
Gadarene
Demoniac

SEA
OF
GALILEE

Galilee
(Jewish)

Decapolis
(pagan)

Tiberias

River
Jordan

| 0 | 1 | | 5 | | 10 Miles |
| 0 | 1 | | 8 | | 16 Kilometres |

7

The Beloved Lake

Dr. Jim Fleming is a fascinating person to talk to. An American Christian, he gained his PhD by developing audio-visual aids to the study of the historical geography of the land of Israel. He is a mine of information on the culture and customs of first-century Galilee. One day we were standing by the Sea of Galilee. 'Don't imagine that the fishermen-disciples of Jesus were poor unskilled men. Galilee fishing was a vital part of the economy of the Middle East. About a thousand boats were engaged on this small stretch of water,' he said, gesturing toward the Lake.

I slipped in a piece of recently acquired knowledge which I rather fancied. 'I've just read that Strabo, the Roman historian, describes the fish from Migdal as very popular in the markets of Rome. Would that be Magdala?'

'That's right. Mary Magdalene, as we call her, was Mary from Migdal, a few miles south of Capernaum. The main fishing centres were Migdal Noonia (Tower of the Fish), Capernaum (Village of Nahum) and Bethsaida (Fish-town). In fact there may have been at least three Bethsaidas! Huge quantities of fresh-water fish still come down from the Upper Jordan into the northern end of the Lake.'

'I'm told that you have come across some old fishermen's tales from the time of Jesus,' I prompted him.

He laughed. 'Yes – the priestly families were particularly keen on fish. One man boasted that he could sit down his guests to a meal of two hundred different kinds of fish.

Another challenges his friends to test his palate. "Catch a
fish anywhere in the land," he says: "cook it and serve it to
me. After one mouthful I shall tell you what kind of fish it is.
After two mouthfuls, I shall tell you where you caught it."
Apparently in those days, the tall tales were told by the men
who ate the fish, not those who caught them!'

I pressed this fascinating man a little further. 'Can we
make any informed guesses about the fishermen Jesus called
to be his disciples?'

'Well, yes. Notice that the brothers Peter and Andrew
worked with Zebedee and his two sons James and John –
plus several hired men and more than one boat (Mark 1:16-
20). That implies quite a large scale business. Now here's
another possible clue. When Jesus was arrested and taken to
the high priest's house, Peter and John were able to get into
the premises because they knew the family (John 18:15).
That *could* imply that "Zebedee, Sons and Partners, Galilee
Fish a Speciality", held the contract to provide fish for the
high-priest's household.'

We strolled along the shore near Capernaum; sometimes
easy walking, and sometimes hard scrambling over black
basalt boulders. Jim pointed to a horseshoe bay about two
hundred yards across. 'Remember how Jesus sat in Peter's
boat and peached to the crowd gathered around the shore?
That's almost certainly the place. As you see, the land forms
a natural amphitheatre. It has been proved possible to talk to
at least ten thousand people here without the aid of amplify-
ing equipment.'

I shielded my eyes from the sun and peered towards the
summit of the rising ground. 'Surely that's the traditional
site of the Sermon on the Mount?'

'Yes, the sound works both ways. People sitting or standing all over the slopes would be able to hear Jesus speaking from the top.'

Called to catch others

We stood and watched modern-day Galilee fishermen trawling off-shore from boats whose general size and shape have not greatly altered since New Testament times. There is no difficulty in saying to yourself 'Jesus stood here'.

Few modern buildings obstruct; in fact the area is less built-up now than it was in his day. I recalled with glee the Sunday school class back in England, whose teacher was relating the incident of the great catch of fish recorded in Luke 5. Having told how Peter, reluctant at first, eventually followed Jesus' bidding and dropped the nets where instinct and experience would tell him there were no prospects, the teacher added, 'What do you think Peter said to Jesus when he found the nets full of fish?' Quick as a flash came back the reply from one cockney lad, who has doubtless gone far by now in street-trading: 'Same time, same place, termorrer!'

In fact, Peter said something quite different: in effect, 'Please keep out of my life'. It was a traumatic moment. A carpenter had just told a fisherman where to catch fish. He was already known to Peter as a rabbi, and more. There was a tussle going on for lordship in Peter's life here; what F. B. Meyer once called 'the settlement as to supreme authority'. A disturbing thought had occurred – 'If this teacher can see to the depths of the lake, perhaps he can see to the depths of my heart. I'm not sure I like that.' So, when Peter saw such a large number of fish, he fell at Jesus' knees and said, 'Go away from me, Lord; I am a sinful man' (Luke 5:8). But Jesus said, 'Don't be afraid; from now on you will catch men.' So they pulled their boats up on shore, left everything and followed him (Luke 5:11).

Is it too much to say that in that incident are found all the principles at work in any man or woman's sense of calling to trust Christ for personal salvation and to follow Christ in public service? An awed sense is awakened that in the figure of Jesus I have met someone very human and yet bigger than any human category; an uncomfortable awareness of my own soiled past and sinful inclinations; a heart tugged two ways at once, away from him and towards him; an inward struggle as to who is really going to run my life, and how many areas of it are going to have to come under his sway – and a conviction, the moment that issue is settled, that if he can do something with even *my* life, then he can do it for anyone and everyone, and that I must take every opportunity to tell them so: 'Follow me – catch men.'

Incidentally, many of the details in these fishing stories are so authentic that we are obviously reading eye-witness accounts and personal memories. It is simply silly to suggest that these are pious myths that have gradually arisen to give expression to spiritual truths. Either these things happened, or the Gospel writers are very clever and deliberate liars: there is no middle choice. Even the different types of fishing nets employed in Galilee are distinguished. Peter and Andrew were using casting-nets (*amphiblestron*) attached to five feet wooden cross-bars, thrown from the beach and drawn back in with cords (Matt. 4:18). James and John were repairing their deep-water drop-nets (*diktna*) when Peter called them across to help (Luke 5:5). During the night they would have been trawling with drag-nets (*sagere*) which Jesus later made into a symbol of the kind of evangelism that catches the attention of many different types of people who will later have to be sorted out (Matt. 13:47).

Jesus' home town

One of my favourite photographs shows Rita and two stran-
gers, man and wife, standing in an arched doorway surrounded by blazing red and violet bougainvillea. Over the
archway, a fading notice announces 'Capernaum – The Town
of Jesus. Open daily, 8.30-16.30'. The wording always
amuses me. I'm so glad that the offer of Christ's gospel does
not close in the mid-afternoon! In fact we talked to that couple, tourists from England, and our conversation about Christ
perhaps bore fruit (or if ours didn't someone else's did), for
several years later we found them eagerly serving Christ in
a pioneer city-centre situation in England.

Kefar Nahum stands empty and silent when the tourists
have left. But so much has been excavated that one can walk
its echoing stone streets past its ruins now only two feet
high, and easily imagine the bustling metropolis, fishing harbour, millstone industry and commercial quarter that was
once indeed Jesus' home town. Here the great *Via Maris*
(road from the Mediterranean) emerged from the Jezreel
Valley and joined the road to the east as it swung around the
north shore of the lake. Here a major taxation centre drew in
the revenue paid reluctantly to the Romans for every article
that was transported through this communications junction.
One of the tax-officers became a disciple of Jesus and used
his shorthand skills to record the words of the Master – Matthew's Gospel. Here the two territories of Herod's rival sons
Antipas and Philippus marched side by side. Here a Roman
garrison lived under its centurions, one of whom had such
respect for the One God of the Jews that he financed the
building of a synagogue, subsequently meeting Jesus and expressing a humble confidence which delighted him and
brought healing to the officer's personal servant (Luke 7:1-10).

Where Jesus taught?

The ruins of a beautiful white fourth-century limestone synagogue just by the fishing quarter are often pointed out as 'the
synagogue of Jesus'. This is a typical piece of tourist shorthand. The building from Jesus' time is actually underneath
the structure – a much simpler building of black basalt with
a rough cobbled floor, perhaps eighty feet long with a colon-
naded community centre and school hall alongside. But only
a hundred yards from it is a more startling discovery. Guides,
as is their wont, casually toss out the claim that they are
pointing to 'St. Peter's house' or 'Jesus' home'. The experienced tourist, having been treated to several dubiously pinpointed sites like this, is inclined to say 'Oh yeah?' and walk
on. That would be a mistake. It is as likely as anything can
be outside the Bible that this is indeed Jesus' home.

In the year 380 AD, Aegeria, a Spanish Christian pilgrim,
visited Capernaum and described a synagogue and a new
church building almost adjoining. The former, 'white with
great steps leading up to it' is clearly the one you can still
see. The church, described as eight-sided, has been recently
built, says the pilgrim, over the ruin of an older house church,
in such a way as to preserve what remains of its walls. That
house church in turn was an enlargement of what the narrator
calls 'the house of the prince of the apostles' (i.e. Peter).

And there it all is, uncovered by the spades of modern
archaeology. An octagonal building is in places oddly arched
over the remains of older walls which in turn show signs of
an earlier building. Mark's Gospel refers no less than eleven
times to the house of Peter's mother-in-law, who was healed
of a fever by Jesus immediately after his first appearance in
the synagogue. This seems to have become Jesus' home and
a kind of Bible-seminary for the first disciples. It was the

normal way for a rabbi to work; gathering between eight and
fifteen disciples who lived with him, served his simple
needs, listened to his table-talk, watched how he handled
people, and privately questioned him about his public teaching. They were encouraged to make personal notes, and to
memorise the teaching. All of these factors suggest fascinating thought about the process that led to the writing of the
four Gospels.[1]

The original floor was found by the excavators to be strewn
with plaster fallen in from the walls. Over a hundred pieces
had graffiti written on them, including references to Peter,
prayers to Jesus, and descriptions of him as the Messiah, the
Most High, the Good and the Lord.

So, the clues fit, the guides are not pulling our legs, and
we are very probably looking at Jesus' adopted home and
the headquarters of the apostolic team. Imagine the scene,
then. The houses in this quarter are *insulae*: extended house-
holds with as many as fifteen rooms (as the family grows by
birth or marriage, you simply add more rooms). Houses were
not so much to *live* in, as to sleep in and store possessions.
Sometimes the house is quiet as the Master gives private
teaching to his little band of disciples (as when he explains
to them the real meaning of the parable of the sower in Matthew 13:2-10). Sometimes the courtyard is packed with a
casually assembled congregation, overflowing into all of the
rooms, which are interconnected by open windows.Once four
men desperate to help their paralysed friend, break through
the simple roof (replaceable every winter) and lower him at
Jesus' feet (Luke 5:18-19). One unforgettable evening, at
least, the adjoining streets are crowded with an excited mob
of the sick, the curious, the troublemakers, the enquirers:
'the whole town was gathered at the door' (Mark 1:32-34).

That immediately followed a startling day when Jesus
had exorcised a demon-possessed man within the synagogue,
then returned to the nearby house and healed Peter's mother-
in-law. Again all of these accounts bear the stamp of eye-
witness memories, not of legends that grew long afterwards.
The scene is right, the customs are correct, the atmosphere
is authentic. Jesus was here: he said these things and
performed these deeds. Quite shortly afterwards, Jews and
Gentiles alike who wished it had never happened, tried to
account for it all in different ways, calling Jesus a magician
or worse. It never seems to have occurred to them to deny
that it all actually happened. They knew better.

Still Christ calls

Back in England, preaching in a Suffolk village chapel, I
tried my best to picture the scene. 'You may say – that is all
very moving and persuasive, but what can it mean to us? We
shall never see Capernaum. We cannot spend three years
with Jesus, listening to his table talk and watching the way
he handles people.'

Several people looked up at me, quite obviously thinking
exactly that. I went on, 'But you needn't say that. For the
very presence of the Holy Spirit means that Jesus will become all to you that he was to his first disciples. You cannot
live with him? But he offers to live with you! "If anyone
hears my voice and opens the door, I will go in and eat with
him and he with me" (Rev. 3:20).

'You cannot listen to his teaching you say? But you can: it
is all recorded by those who first heard it. Read the Gospel
narratives, part of God's inspired Word. "Ah, but I cannot
question him privately about its meaning," you say. But you
can do that, too. Make a daily appointment with him: read

the Bible, and pray that he will explain its meaning to you. Millions do it every day.

'And what about that wonderful experience of watching how he handles people? That is exactly what you begin to do when you really come into the fellowship of the church.

'Don't just "go to church" but give time and trouble to the gathering of God's believing people, worshipping with them, sharing your discoveries, praying for each other, listening to each other's experiences. All over the place, churches are waking up to what this means. Get into it and discover it for yourself.'

We had a moment of silent prayer in the little chapel, and then three people indicated their desire to know the living Christ. One said to me next time I met him, 'I listened fascinated, and thought – "*This is real, but it can't be for me.*" Then, when you prayed, my heart began to thump, and I started to sweat, and I thought, "*Either I'm having a heart-attack, or I'm getting converted.*" Well – I got converted!'

Jesus still calls us,

> ...o'er the tumult
> of the world's wild restless sea,
> Day by day His sweet voice soundeth,
> Saying, Christian, follow Me.
>
> As of old, apostles heard it,
> By the Galilean lake
> Turned from home and toil and kindred
> Leaving all for His dear sake. [2]

Sadly, in my opinion, the Fransiscans have recently built a particularly ghastly chapel over the site of 'Peter's House'. It stands on stone stilts, like some alien space craft from Wells' *War of the Worlds*. Its one important virtue is that the stilts allow visitors to peer down at the ancient remains

below, which for years have been hidden behind protective
screens. There is always some blessing to be found in
Capernaum!

Twentieth-century disciples

A group of Jewish young adults asked to talk to me. Someone had pointed me out, as I paddled barefoot along the sea-
shore, as 'that preacher from Jerusalem'. They told me of
their faith in Jesus, and the high price they had to pay for it.
Most Israelis have an attitude of live-and-let-live, but not
the ultra-orthodox. These very earnest and vociferous enthusiasts are in direct line from the Pharisees of Jesus' day and
I've heard more than one secular Israeli refer to them precisely in those terms. Some of them had employed a species
of religious Scargillism to prevent the Messianic Believers
of Galilee from worshipping. A hundred had turned up one
Sabbath morning, jeering and threatening the worshippers in
their little hall. Next week it was five hundred, and the next
a thousand. They promised five thousand the following Sabbath. At that point the local mayor, himself a *hassid*, closed
the meeting-hall as a potential cause of trouble.

The followers of Jesus 'went underground' meeting somewhere different each week, by prior arrangement. Yet such
is the attractiveness of their faith, and such is the reality of
the presence of Jesus amongst them, that Jews, Arabs and
Gentiles attach themselves to their little group and in turn
put their faith in the Saviour.

There is a lovely Scottish Hospice at Tiberius, Herod's
Galilee capital apparently never visited by Jesus. The Church
of Scotland has a chapel there and the hospice (i.e. pilgrim's
guest house) is a series of black stone buildings just back

from the shore. Originally a hospital, it stands in fine grounds
full of the whole blaze and glory of Galilee trees, shrubs and
flowers. Josephus wrote lyrically of the local vegetation:

> Thanks to the rich soil, there is not a plant that does not flourish;
> the air is so temperate that it suits the most diverse varieties. The
> winter-loving walnut grows luxuriously beside the palm which
> thrives on heat, and side by side with the fig and the olive. One
> might deem it nature's crowning ambition to place together in a
> single spot the most discordant species in healthy rivalry.[3]

The Talmud, with pardonable exaggeration, assures us that
fruit grew as rapidly as the deer runs, and the fruit is so light
and sweet that a man can eat a hundred pieces and not feel
full.

To the Jewish sages, in fact, Galilee was the Beloved
Lake. When God made the seven seas, they tell us, he pronounced them good. But when he made Galilee, he found his
delight. To that, every Christian will say a hearty *amen*, for
here we have found *our* delight too – the One of whom the
Father bore witness in the words: 'This is my beloved Son,
in whom is all my delight' (Luke 3:22).

The Church of Scotland does not attempt mission work
amongst Jews or Arabs seeing itself rather as a provision
for expatriate Christians. Nevertheless, the efficiency of their
establishment, the sense of vocation expressed by the staff
and the preaching heard at the chapel, bear gentle witness to
Jesus. I heard from a burly Scottish minister one of the finest
expositions I have ever heard of what the Puritans used to
call 'The Glorious Exchange' from the apostle's great words:
'God made him (Jesus) who had no sin to be sin for us, so
that in him we might become the righteousness of God'
(2 Cor. 5:21).

Nearby, Avner Ram, one of Israel's finest professional guides with an encyclopaedic knowledge of the Bible, showed me the hot springs of Tiberius. They are back in use, offering treatment for skin disorders and rheumatic illnesses. Their presence accounted for Herod's decision to build one of his many palaces there (with a gold roof, it was said). It also explains what often puzzled me as a child hearing the Bible stories. Why did everyone around Galilee seem to be *sick*? Now I know. Because Galilee was where the sick went: the Bath or the Harrogate, or one might also say the Lourdes, of the ancient Middle East.

One tradition stated that if a leper knelt all night in one of the streams, fell asleep and dreamed, then he would awaken cured. As in the New Testament, 'leprosy' was a rather imprecise word meaning any disfiguring skin disease, and was not used exclusively to describe the appalling disease for which a cure has only recently been found.

Interestingly, the two men whom Jesus healed in quick succession at Capernaum represented the two ailments which most regularly drove sufferers to Galilee (Luke 5:12-19). Sandwiched between the call of four disciples to leave their fishing and the call of another to leave his tax-collecting, the whole string of stories bear unintended and coincidental witness to the total accuracy of Luke's account of the way of life prevalent around Capernaum.

Last time I met Avie, at Easter 1995, he took me to the only recently discovered Korazin. This was one of the three towns that drew Jesus' particular reproach because of their unbelief, in spite of the many miracles performed there (Korazin, Bethsaida and Capernaum, Matt. 11:20-24). It perches high on the hillside, and therefore at about sea-level! The archaeologists are now rebuilding some of the structures with the original stones, including the synagogue, which apparently had a magnificent view of the lake from the doorstep. The 'pulpit' has been found: actually a stone seat (see Luke 4:20-21). With complete certainty we can say, 'Jesus taught here.'

The boat that came back

From 1984 to 1986 there were drought conditions in Galilee, and the level of the lake dropped severely. Two Israeli brothers from a nearby kibbutz were hopefully exploring the enlarged shore when they found forty ancient coins scattered in the mud. Digging around for more, they came across fragments of wood and the obvious outline of a boat. Events moved rapidly, with that mixture of zany humour, religious excitement, eye for the main chance and glorious exaggeration which are typical ingredients of life in modern Israel.

The brothers dutifully reported their find to the authorities, who tried to keep the lid on it, since digging holes and finding things is a popular hobby. Unfortunately someone 'leaked' and hordes of hopefuls with spades began to scour the shore. Decoy holes were hurriedly dug and then half covered so as to mislead people. The television people turned up. Rumour had it that 'the boat of Jesus' had been discovered. The Minister of Tourism, quick to see the possibilities announced a 'major Christian relic' and started taking tenders for the building of a 'shrine'!

Ultra-orthodox Jews organised more demonstrations, claiming that the whole thing was a con-trick organised by missionaries (the worst thing they can call anybody). A party of Christian Eskimos arrived from Alaska, clamouring to see it.

As the drought ended and the water rose, a race against

time developed to prise the wreck loose, lift it clear without destroying it, and then preserve it, bearing in mind the delicacy of the wood which was eighty per cent waterlogged. The kind of skills employed on the Tudor ship *Mary Rose* in England were invoked, and the water-content of the wood was gradually replaced with polyethylene glycol, which eventually solidifies.

Of course the craft does fall short of being Jesus' boat (or even Peter's boat) but it is a unique example of the kind of little ship that appears in the Gospels. The age is roughly right. The boat is thirty feet long, rather tubby (seven feet wide) and distinctly shallow (four feet deep). It reminds me, in shape and size, of a Yorkshire 'cobble'. The planks are held together by mortise-and-tenon joints (simply – pegs in one plank, holes in the next). It was part-decked and propelled by one sail and three or four pairs of oars. Most strikingly, it closely resembles a Christian mosaic of a boat from the earliest centuries, already found outside nearby Migdal. A few objects were still inside the ruined craft: arrowheads, net-weights, a cooking pot, an oil lamp.

Meeting Christ on the beach

Not long before the boat was found, a group of us stood on the shore north of Migdal and just short of Capernaum. By ancient tradition, the little shingle beach is the place where Jesus met his fishermen-disciples after his death and resurrection (John 21). It could well be so.

Half of the events we associate with his ministry happened in an amazingly small area. You can row a mile offshore and take one photograph which will encompass most of it.

At some time in the past, pious folk have laid six great flat heart-shaped stones across the tiny beach and into the water. They represent, one assumes, the thrice-repeated question of Jesus to Peter, 'Lovest thou me?' (John 21:15-17) and the three replies. Thirty of us stood on the fine shingle, as little ripples splashed and played over the stones. A fishing boat was anchored a hundred yards off-shore; just the correct distance to illustrate the story. I read the matchless tale and commented on it.

Clearly the whole incident was carefully stage-managed by Jesus. Every detail was set up to stir memories and awaken consciences. Every scene in the act was a replay of previous occasions. An unrecognised stranger shows men who have fished unsuccessfully all night where to catch fish – and the nets are filled: a replay of that unforgettable scene when he first called them. Bread and fish await them by a lake as Jesus distributes the food: a replay of the feeding of the five thousand. A *charcoal* fire (*anthracion*) burns; the word is only used once elsewhere: 'It was cold, and the servants and officials stood around an *anthracion* they had made to keep warm. Peter was standing with them, warming himself...' (John 18:18).

He warmed himself at the world's fire, and was soon denying his Lord (as we invariably do, if that's the warmth we seek). Now Jesus invites Peter to warm himself at his fire, and pick up the task of discipleship once more.

And, of course, I read the famous three questions.

'Peter, do you *love* me more than these?' (with *agape* – deep unshaken, divine love).

'Well, Lord, you know that I'm very fond of you' (*philia*).

'Peter – do you truly *love* me?'

'Well, Lord, we are *friends* – I dare to say that.'

'All right, Peter – let's start where you can honestly start. Are we *friends*, then?'

'Master, you know my heart, you know we are.'

'Then from that modest beginning, I can fan the flames of friendship into deep, divine love, so that you give a lifetime to tending my sheep and feeding my lambs – and then go willingly to a martyr's death.'

So we might paraphrase the moving exchange.

I paused on the question that Bible-readers sometimes discuss. 'Do you truly love me *more than these*?' asked Jesus. More than who? Or what? Perhaps 'more than these fish' since the bewildered disciples, not knowing what else to do after those traumatic events, had surely taken a backwards step in returning to their fishing.

Or perhaps 'more than these other disciples' since only a few days ago Peter had insisted that even if all the others abandoned Jesus, *he* wouldn't – and with what a pathetic follow-through.

Douglas was one of our party, a big man, owner of a business in England. Owner, too, of a splendid camera, with which he had come to Israel with the intention of taking first-class pictures. Until the security men at the airport examined it – and accidentally broke it! Douglas had tried everywhere to get it repaired. Not a chance. For several days he was really angry and frustrated as a succession of breathtaking views and marvellous sunsets mocked his inability to capture any of them on film. Now as I finished my little homily, he approached me trembling with emotion.

'Do you love me *more than these*?' he quoted. 'It has just dawned on me that I've been missing the whole point of the trip to Israel. This isn't a place to take nice pictures; it's the place where Christ walked. Do you know, Don, as you read that story, it seemed to me Jesus was saying to me, "Douglas, do you love me *more than these photographs*?" Well –

I want to get clear once and for all who is running my life. Would you baptise me?'

I was glad to. This was no spur-of-the-moment decision and I knew it. Next day we baptised Douglas in the river Jordan, where it flows out of the lake, together with his daughter Ruth, along with several others who had for some time been approaching a serious commitment to Christ.

Douglas subsequently sold his business, and worked unpaid in various ways, for the Belgian Evangelical Mission, One Step Forward, and The Evangelization Society. Ruth took training with Moorlands Bible College and now works as a Wycliffe Bible Translator in Burkina Faso, where Africans in large numbers are turning from animism to follow the Christ of Galilee.

> Jesus calls us from the worship
> Of the vain world's golden shore,
> From each idol that would keep us,
> Saying, 'Christian love Me more? '

References

1. Donald Bridge, *Jesus, the Man and His Message*, Christian Focus Publications, 1995, chap. 5.
2. Hymn, 'Jesus calls us o'er the tumult', Cecil Frances Alexander, 1818-95.
3. Josephus, *The Wars of the Jews*, Book 3: Chapter 10, para. 8, p. 25. Newly translated with commentary and notes, General editor Gaalya Cornfield, Zondervan, 1982.

8

Not Like the Scribes

Susan Marcos is undoubtedly one of Israel's best professional guides. Jewish-American by background, she and her family have paid a high price for making alliyah back to Israel. All of them need to work long hard hours to make ends meet. One son has lost a leg in the Israeli Defence Force. One of her poems asks:

> To what have we come?
> This land, desolate, neglected:
> Tears of sand fill dry riverbeds.
> Suddenly a bloom, a blade of grass
> Quickens the heart of the soil
> Already soaked with the blood of centuries.
>
> Was it always thus?
> Trails of awesome pen and power
> Boom and roll over the same roads our ancestors walked.

Susan and I have walked together over those 'same roads' following the footprints of Jesus. We had a simple arrangement. At each place where Jesus had spoken and acted, she would sketch, for our tourists, the background of custom, culture and religion. Then I gave the Christian implications. For example, she described a house with its low walls and tiled or turfed roof, and showed how easily a paralysed man could be lowered through the roof at Jesus' feet (Mark 2:1-5). Then I expounded the impact of Jesus' amazing words to the cripple, 'Your sins are forgiven. Rise up and walk.' As Susan smilingly noncommittal, said on one such occasion, 'There's the humanity of Jesus – now over to Don for the deity!'

As we walked along a ruler-straight road in the Jezreel valley, the surrounding fields thick with produce (for he who claimed to be the Bread of Life hailed from the vale known as the bread-basket of Israel), Susan explained how an itinerant rabbi lived and worked. With his dozen or so disciples he tramped from village to village, carrying his sheepskin diploma of rabbinical training. Warned by sharp eyed small boys, the people would pour out to meet him, still well outside the village, and the 'preaching' would begin immediately as the excited noisy procession covered the last mile. Not for nothing is Luke's Gospel patterned as a seemingly endless walking-tour.

At first sight Jesus must have resembled a typical travelling rabbi, except that he had no sheepskin diploma, as was scornfully pointed out – 'The Jews were amazed and asked, "How did this man get such learning without having studied?"' (John 7:15).

But the more he talked, the more it became evident that this was no ordinary rabbi. Susan's emphasis on 'humanity' and mine on 'deity' became bewilderingly intertwined. 'When Jesus had finished saying these things, the crowds were amazed at his teaching, because he taught as one who had authority, and not as their teachers of the law' (Matt. 7:28-29). What did they mean? Surely it was supposed to be the official teachers who had the authority and Jesus who was unauthorised?

They were referring to his style. The job of the scribes was to hunt down matters of fact and precedent in the huge collection of written and oral tradition, often to settle some social or legal dispute. The Pharisees went further and tried to interpret and apply the material to moral and religious issues. Their method was to quote some Bible incident, then

invoke a number of varying interpretations of it – what rabbi
so-and-so said about it three hundred years ago – what (on
the other hand) my rabbi thought it meant when I asked him
ten years ago – what a recent court-case decided on the point
– what a line in one of the psalms says that may possibly
have some bearing on it – and by the way, I heard a story the
other day – and so on, almost *ad infinitum*. Much of this was
purely oral in Jesus' time, and referred to as the tradition of
the elders. Within another four hundred years (with all the
further additions and comments of those centuries) it was
encapsulated in the Mishnah and then further in the Talmud,
a collection of mind-numbing complexity which you can take
a life-time to find your way around. I've often lingered
outside the window of a yeshiva (study-school) and watched
men young and old raising hypothetical questions, scurrying
from one scroll to another to find precedents, chanting
quotations, and loudly taking up opposing positions.

Jesus dismissed some of this (not all) in terse words. 'Some
Pharisees and teachers of the law asked Jesus, "Why do your
disciples break the tradition of the elders? They don't wash their
hands before they eat"' (Matt. 15:1). (This was not a matter
of hygiene, but of scrupulously following a developed ritual
of ceremonial washing and blessings.)

Jesus replied, 'And why do you break the command of God
for the sake of your tradition? .... You nullify the word of God
for the sake of your tradition!' He goes on to take two typical
examples of the process in which a welter of comments and
customs simply obscure the plain meaning of God's com-
mands (Matt. 15:1-12).

The authority which Jesus displayed, therefore, was his
manner of cutting through human traditions to the plain
meaning of God's word – or shining dazzling new light on

its implications. And the simple stark formula that went with it? 'I say unto you.' That is authority! The certainty of someone with words from God.

Sunshine in Nazareth

My pulpit one Sunday was a carpenter's bench. What could be more appropriate on a Nazareth hilltop in the chapel of a Christian hospital? Visible behind my shoulder as I preached was a panoramic view of Jesus' home town, and in the far distance the mountain village of Nain. Jesus interrupted the funeral of a widow's son up there. In the very same area Elisha, eight centuries earlier, had done the same for another widow's son (Luke 7:11-17 and 2 Kgs. 8). In both cases those who received God's kindness were non-Jews. That fact, underlined by Jesus in this same town of Nazareth, so infuriated his hearers that they tried to lynch him (Luke 4:24-30). Curious how newcomers to an exclusive club can in turn become passionate defenders of its closed shop! For Galileans were not racially true Jews. A polyglot people of pagan origins, forcibly settled long ago by a dictator to replace the 'lost' tribes of Israel, they had been converted by force to the Jewish faith during the brief halcyon days of Jewish political independence under the Maccabees, around 120-100 BC. Jerusalemites regarded them with amused contempt rather than the hatred that they held for the Samaritans, whose origins were similar, but who had a rival temple (John 4:19-24). However the Galileans differed from Samaritans in that their conversion to Judaism was more complete, and their population was supplemented by immigration of Jewish exiles back from Babylon and Persia. Nazareth gained its name from the settlement of such a group who could trace their ancestry back to David.[1]

Rita and I bought some luscious fruit in the Nazareth street market at a ludicrously low price, and ate it gratefully in the blazing heat of midday, squatting on a flat stone beside the ancient synagogue which stands on the site of Jesus' famous sermon. The glorious melody of his words ran through our minds as we recalled it. Not his own words, in fact, but a quotation from Isaiah 61.

> The Spirit of the LORD is on me because he has anointed me to preach good news to the poor. He has sent me to proclaim freedom for the prisoners and recovery of sight for the blind, to release the oppressed, to proclaim the year of the LORD's favour (Isa. 61:1-2).

The fiftieth year

Rita had become intrigued by the subject of the Year of Jubilee. This astonishing and neglected Old Testament teaching proposes a national slate-wiping exercise at fifty year intervals. Debts are to be cancelled, slaves released, and property returned to those families compelled by poverty to sell it. In one simple stroke, the principal causes of social injustice, class warfare and revolution, were banished at regular intervals.

We made two startling discoveries. The synagogues did in fact have a lectionary – a set of Scripture readings linked with the calendar. Jesus presumably turned to the set reading for that Sabbath in Galilee. But in that calendar, Leviticus 25 is linked with Isaiah 61. And Leviticus 25 is the Jubilee command.[2] This connection is obvious, once you have the clue. Jubilee is all about new beginnings; Isaiah's Messiah offers such a new start; Jesus brings new life. Jubilee rescued the poor from their poverty; Isaiah brings good news to the poor; Jesus promises the Kingdom to the poor in spirit. Jubilee emptied the prisons, Isaiah proclaims freedom for the prisoner, Jesus sets the captive free.

That was our first discovery. The second followed on its heels. It is widely assumed that Israel never seriously attempted the ideal of Jubilee. (Incidentally, what would modern monetarism make of the system? The imagination boggles!) Only nominal attempts were made to observe it. Certainly the calculations were kept up, and the Jubilee Year marked in some way. And here comes the shock. Assuming that Jesus was born in 4 BC, his public ministry must have begun in the year 26 AD – which was due to be the next Year of Jubilee![3]

A synagogue sensation

We gazed at the locked door of the Nazareth synagogue, and in imagination pictured the scene behind it. Every Jubilee pointed on to the Jubilee (in Jewish minds) when Messiah would bring, not merely a one-year social readjustment, but the New Age.

'Then he rolled up the scroll, gave it back to the attendant and sat down. The eyes of everyone in the synagogue were fastened on him, and he said to them, "Today this scripture is fulfilled in your hearing"' (Luke 4:20-21). No wonder they said, 'Who's this?' And no wonder they winced when, having made the stunning claim to be Israel's Messiah, he apparently snatched it back from them with irritating words about non-Jews getting the benefits!

We sat in silence. There were so many avenues to explore. Was Jubilee, a clue to all that teaching about trust and worry, about physical needs and eyes set on God's Kingdom? After all, identical words are used. 'You may ask, "What will we eat in the seventh year if we do not plant or harvest our crops?"' (Lev. 25:20). A practical enough question, when the fiftieth year inevitably followed a forty-ninth which was a Sabbath rest for the land left uncultivated for twelve months.

The question is echoed – and answered – by Jesus: 'Do not set your heart on what you will eat or drink: do not worry about it .... seek God's Kingdom, and these things will be given to you as well' (Luke 12:29-31).

Those odd parables about a rich man's steward who cheerfully cancels his employer's credit-notes – and a banker who waïves enormous debts – to say the least, they start to fit into a new scenario in 26 AD. Was Jesus saying 'God's Jubilee has come – in me. Be ready for the radical life-style to which I call you. Put God's Kingdom first'? It is a point to which every Christian traveller in Israel returns again and again. The teaching of Jesus (as distinct from his cross and resurrection) is at the same time a radical call to a single, trustful life-style, and an immensely complex labyrinth of Old Testament allusions, prophetic promises with undreamt-of meanings, and towering personal claims. He may never have said in so many words, 'I am God' (the phrase in the Jewish Middle East would be so shocking as to be incomprehensible and without meaning). But in a hundred different ways by implication, that is exactly what he was saying. What else when he embraces every Old Testament title of God? Shepherd, judge, king, physician, jubilee, rock, light, bride-groom, vineyard-owner, saviour, foundation, life-giver. Who is this?

Theology and culture

Two of us were scrambling over the olive-studded slopes of the Judaean hills overlooking Galilee. The olive leaves shimmered in the breeze with rippling waves of pale green and silver. My companion was a Christian theologian of high repute. He had just tossed out a provocative remark. 'You know, Paul wasn't the first theologian but the second – Jesus was the first.'

Dr. Kenneth Bailey has two unusual qualifications. He has worked for five years in a literacy team, living in isolated Arabic villages that have remained virtually unchanged since Jesus' time. He has spent a lifetime pastoring small Christian congregations in similar remote areas of Egypt and Lebanon. His Bible teaching has therefore been aimed at a society and culture almost identical to that of Jesus' day. The attitudes, values, customs, relationships and responses of these Arab congregations are the same as those of Jesus' hearers. This has enabled him to explore the art of storytelling within the culture in which Jesus told his parables.

As we walked, I contributed what little knowledge I could boast. 'The man who declined to follow Jesus until he had buried his father is an example, isn't it? I think most of us even in the west suspect that his father hadn't actually died.'

'No, of course not,' smiled Dr. Bailey. 'To bury your father means to put off major decisions and changes in lifestyle until you have become the heir and the head of the family – maybe in ten, fifteen years' time. Incidentally, the similar story that goes with that one – the young man who asks permission to run home and say goodbye to his family before he joined the disciples – that one really is a shocker. To say goodbye or beg leave, means to call a family conference and have a lengthy discussion, after which the family gives permission for you to leave home. Jesus brushed all that aside and said, "Make up your own mind, come now." I've actually seen Lebanese students go white-faced with shock as I told the story. It implies the claim of Jesus to over-ride the most rigid family rights. Only God can make such a claim.'

He warmed to his theme, as we ate pitta bread, cheese and dates, in the shade of a eucalyptus tree.

'You see, the truths that come repeatedly in the Gospel

episodes and the parables are always very much the same. The absolute priority of the Kingdom of God, the unique authority of Jesus, the astonishing free grace of God extended to the undeserving – and all of it a contradiction of the Pharisees' philosophy of salvation by religious merit, with their judging of people by external criteria – what you wear, customs you follow, rituals you perform, and so on. You see what I mean by Jesus the theologian? We westerners with our logic and our analogies think of Paul as the supreme thinker and theologian. He represents the great arguments – the doctrines of grace – and then we go back to the Jesus-narratives and parables for illustrations. But they are not the illustrations. They are the theology. Paul's doctrines are the illustrations!'

I mused as we finished our scratch meal and strolled back towards Capernaum. Often, I recalled, a parable arose out of a scene which already had controversy and drama in it. The delightful little tale of the two debtors, for example (Luke 7:41-43). I've often preached from it, seeing it as an illustration of justification by faith and salvation by grace. But of course Kenneth Bailey was right. It wasn't just an illustration it was the thing itself. Some of the details I knew from Edersheim.[4] Others I now checked with Kenneth. It is interesting to take a look at the complete passage in which this parable appears (Luke 7:36-50) to get a better idea of its context.

Simon the Pharisee invited Jesus home to a meal, presumably after hearing him preach. The room would be open along one side to the passing public.

First shock: the host provides his guest with no water and no foot-washing. That was not an oversight, but, a calculated insult. Simon hadn't enjoyed the sermon!

Second shock: a woman in the crowd following, is incensed by the insult. She has presumably been deeply moved by Jesus' preaching. She pushes in and takes over the neglected duty. Tears of gratitude and penitence provide the missing water, and her hair does duty for the missing towel. But, for a woman to unbind her hair is an intimate action, performed only before her husband in the bedroom. Onlookers look embarrassed, hiss and avert their eyes.

Third shock: she produces perfume which she has been carrying. Its purpose is normally to attract customers – for she is by this time recognised as one of the community's prostitutes (known to everyone in a small town, reviled, loathed, unclean, and of course quietly used).

Fourth shock: Simon is revolted and angry. But Jesus, looking into her eyes, and addressing her, not Simon, praises her action and condemns his inaction.

Fifth shock: He tells a simple parable which, in its Eastern idiom announces two amazing facts. She has found God's free forgiveness, and Simon the righteous is still in his sin. Love and goodness spring from free pardon.

New light on the Prodigal Son

Later, in a study-group for Anglican workers, we sat breathlessly whilst Dr. Bailey gave a more detailed demonstration. We looked at that most famous of parables: the Prodigal Son (Luke 15:11-32). It is, of course, the parable of free forgiveness. And therein lies a problem. Those who dislike the evangelical understanding of forgiveness at a price (the price of the cross) are quick to point out with glee that it cannot be found in this parable. The runaway is forgiven simply because he is sorry and comes home. There is no mediator, no atonement, no saviour. The price of the lad's folly is paid by him, amongst the pigs, and in the reality of his repentance.

'Wrong,' said our instructor, and continued his riveting exposition of the Prodigal's story. (I paraphrase from now onwards, but all of this and very much more can be found in one of Kenneth Bailey's scholarly books.[5])

Put the story back where it belongs; back in the peasant village, and it becomes the story of the Father's suffering. The son's demand for his inheritance before his father's death was a devastating insult to his father and a crude defiance of the whole extended family of villagers. (Every peasant community questioned by Bailey agreed.)

First, the request meant in effect, 'drop dead, Dad.'

Second, the father should have replied with a blow on the face and a public statement, 'From now on you are dead.'

Third, the whole community would take scandalised action. A custom called qesasah made provision for 'cutting off' any villager who sold his inheritance to Gentiles (which is what the son did in the far country).[6]

Later, the young man is in dire need. He comes to his senses and decides to return rather than starve. He has two problems to face. He has insulted and robbed his father. Maybe he can do something about that. He will offer to work as a hired servant (living in the village, but not at home). His wages can gradually be saved to at least partly repay his debt ('Make me like one of your hired men'). It is a perfect example of the Pharisees' understanding of repentance, which is essentially salvation by works – you earn God's forgiveness by prayer, almsgiving and penitence. Simon the Pharisee would have approved of the lad's new intentions so far!

So the problem of the father may perhaps be settled that way. The problem of the village really has no answer: it will just have to be faced.

Word of his return will flash around. A mob will gather with shouts, threats and blows. He will have to run the gauntlet, in fact. He could even be killed.

But what actually happens? The father sees his prodigal returning, and hurries out of the village to meet him. He runs the gauntlet, to give his protection to his son. But an oriental man of property never runs: to do so is grievously to demean himself in society's eyes. Moreover, running is only physically possible by hitching up his tight ankle-length robe and revealing his long underpants! Shouts of anger turns to hoots of ribald mirth in the crowd. The father is suffering for the wanderer.

They meet, and the son begins his 'let's make a bargain: I'll start to work and pay' speech. The father interrupts it with wordless kisses, the gift of his own festal robe, the presentation of his own signet ring, and an order for sandals to be put on his feet. The robe would symbolise to any oriental audience imputed character, the ring delegated authority, and the sandals a promise that the youth who last time went out in shame from his father will soon go out on commissions for his father. I have several times preached a sermon solely on those three articles and seen lives radically changed by the implications. A converted jailbird immediately took up the point of the sandals, returned to the prison as a visitor, and led three inmates to Christ. 'I've been wearing the shoes, like you said,' he reported to me.

The community is still to be reconciled. By now the villagers will be stunned into amazed silence. Father orders an animal to be slain. Killing an animal for the sake of a guest goes far beyond mere hospitality. It is a 'blood covenant' between host and guest. The guest physically steps over the blood at the threshold, into a sacred unbreakable covenant-relationship, witnessed by the village.[7] Moreover, the killing of a small cow (food for a hundred people) is an invitation to the whole community to join in the feast that follows. The father's public words 'you are alive' when he should have said 'you are dead' are now fortified by a command to the whole village, 'Come and join in the great reconciliation.'

Which neatly brings the end of the parable back to its beginning, which was a scandalised complaint by the Pharisees that Jesus 'welcomes sinners and eats with them' (verses 1-2). Gospel and church are here: Ephesians 2 illustrates it, but Jesus has already theologised it.

The rabbi from Nazareth has presented, in almost shocking form, a totally new concept of repentance. It is the acceptance of a completely free and undeserved offer of pardon, sonship, and membership of God's community. The price is paid by God. Is there no cross in the Prodigal Son?

References
1. See Bargil Pixner, *With Jesus Through Galilee, according to the fifth Gospel*, Corazin, 1992.
2. Rabbi Stephen Schwarzschild in correspondence with John Howard Yoder. Yoder, *The Politics of Jesus*, Eerdmans: USA, 1972, p. 37.
3. Yoder, *ibid*, pp. 65-76.
4. Alfred Edersheim, *The Life and Times of Jesus the Messiah*.
5. Kenneth Bailey, *Poet and Peasant*, Eerdmans: Michigan USA, 1976, pp. 158-162.
6. A. M. Rihbany, *The Syrian Christ*, Houghton Mifflin: Boston, 1916. Quoted at length by K Bailey, *ibid*, pp. 186-187.
7. I explore the significant reason *why* Jesus told the parable, and the importance of 'eating with sinners' in my *Jesus, the Man and His Message*, Christian Focus Publications, 1995 (chapter 3, The Man Who Broke Barriers) and in my *Why Four Gospels?*, Mentor, 1996 (chapter 12, Eating With Sinners).

9

The Donkey and the Tank

Rita and I were engaged in a favourite exercise. We retraced the Palm Sunday ride of Jesus, from Bethpage, down the western slope of the Mount of Olives, across Kedron, and up to the Golden Gate. Two scenes in sharp contrast suddenly confronted us. A huge military tank, gun reversed, rumbled down the Jericho road, part of the pull-out from Lebanon. And a man rode past it on a donkey. 'Behold your king comes, meek and lowly, riding on a donkey' (Zech. 9:9).

What a commentary on that extraordinary last week which began when Jesus of Nazareth mounted the lowly beast and rode with his homely entourage of country folk putting on their pathetic demo, with leafy branches their only banners. To the Roman sentries it meant nothing, to the Jews everything. But for both there was being played out the cosmic struggle for power: the seemingly endless conflict for the loyalties of humanity. Here the Man on the donkey confronted the man in the tank – and won the crown.

Approaching the city

Jesus had walked about a hundred miles from Galilee. With three miles to go, why did he suddenly want to ride? Deliberate purpose and deep symbolism was here, as his careful instructions imply (Luke 19:29-31). Bethpage, just over the crest of the hill from Bethany, had recently become the official border of the city. Standing three miles outside the actual city walls, the little cluster of houses was the equivalent of a road sign proclaiming, 'Jerusalem – city of

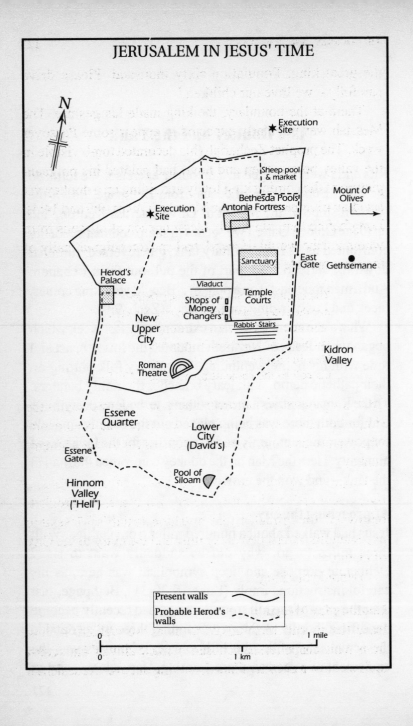

JERUSALEM IN JESUS' TIME

N

★ Execution Site

Sheep pool & market

Bethesda Pools
Antonia Fortress

Mount of Olives →

★ Execution Site

Sanctuary

East Gate

● Gethsemane

Herod's Palace

Viaduct

Shops of Money Changers

Temple Courts

Rabbis' Stairs

New Upper City

Kidron Valley

Roman Theatre

Essene Quarter

Lower City (David's)

Essene Gate

Pool of Siloam

Hinnom Valley ("Hell")

Present walls
Probable Herod's walls

0   1 mile

0   1 km

the great king. Population sixty thousand. Please drive carefully – we love our children.'

There at the boundary, the king made his gesture. The Messiah was popularly expected to appear some Passover week. The prophet Zechariah (his decorated tomb visible in the valley below, then and now) had painted his poignant picture of the coming king lowly and riding on a donkey yet standing triumphant upon the Mount of Olives (9:9 and 14:4). Long before that, old Jacob, blessing each of his sons from whom a tribe would descend, had spoken enigmatically of the same humble animal.

> The sceptre will not depart from Judah
> nor the ruler's staff from between his feet,
> until he comes to whom it belongs, and
> the obedience of the nations is his.
> He will tether his donkey to a vine
> his colt to the choicest branch (Gen. 49:10).

That is a picture of prosperity and power, expressed in the simple terms of a nomad. For how prosperous is someone who can use one of his vines as a tethering-post for a hungry donkey!

King, ruler's staff, sceptre, obedience of the nations.... Every Jew knew what this meant, when a rabbi-prophet, renowned for miracles that outshine Isaiah's Messianic expectations, at last declares himself at the entry to the City of David.

'Behold your king!'

Looking for Messiah

Isaac (let us call him) talked to us as we walked. A Jew from Whitechapel, he had chosen to 'make alliyah' and return to Zion. Now a citizen of Israel, looking out over Jerusalem's turmoil of competing religious, political and military pressures, he opened his heart to me.

'When a Jew comes back, there are four possible ways open to him. There is *Zionism*: redemption through return to the land. We thought our problems would be over then, but they were only beginning. We have to hold the land by force and exhaust our economy to do it. Nothing is solved.

'There is *Secularism*. Most Israelis have no religion. But this turns out to be barren and empty. Our youth has a huge disillusionment problem and drugs are an epidemic.

'There is *Religion*. That seems the obvious way. After all, what is a Jew, if not a religious man? But we look at religious orthodoxy and we see legalism, bigotry, harshness.

'That leaves *Messiah* as the final option. We've always said, half jokingly, "When Messiah comes" meaning "probably never". Like your old English phrase, "When my ship comes in". But now we are desperate for him to come. Did you know that Israeli youths have stickers that say in Hebrew "*Messiah Now*?"

'Messiah! But you see that raises a new problem. For you cannot think of Messiah for very long, without this terrible thought arising: *What more could Messiah be than Jesus of Nazareth is already?* Well – as for me – I have made my choice. Recently I was baptised in the name of Yeshua H'amashiah (Jesus the Messiah). Now I have been found – for he has found me.'

No fruit on the fig-tree

We lingered at Bethany, discovering to our delight a donkey in a sloping stone-filled field, tethered by a long rope to the doorpost. We thoughtfully fingered the dusty leaves and unripe fruit of a fig-tree. It was hereabouts that Jesus performed that strange act of withering the fig-tree (Mark 11:12-14).

It puzzles the modern reader. How could it be expected to yield fruit if 'it was not the season for figs'? In fact it could and should. As soon as leaves appear, the little green nutritious 'pages' (pronounced 'pargees') should be there too. The season for figs is the time for picking the ripened fruit (two months or more later). But for a hungry man, the pages made acceptable food: if there were none by this time, there would be none this year. And was not the whole area renowned for its little unripe figs? Bethpage means 'the place of little figs'. So – a name for fruitfulness, but no fruit. Hypocrisy, in fact. This is what Jesus 'curses' (although it is Peter, not Jesus, who actually uses that ugly word).

An Israeli friend led us through the garden of the Paternoster Church on the outskirts of Bethpage. So-called because of the Lord's Prayer inscribed on the walls in seventy different languages, the building hides another spectacle which most tourists miss. There is the usual succession of ruins below the church – a Crusader building from the eleventh century, a Byzantine chapel from the seventh – and then a little walled-in cave with traces of worship and burial in the very earliest days of Jewish Christianity. Here is a deeply moving possibility. Jesus had some favourite spot on the summit of Olivet where he often taught (Matt. 24:3; John 8:1), with the breathtaking view of Jerusalem stretched below. Was this the place? Christians in the fourth century certainly thought so, and showed it to the mother of the first Christian emperor. Even earlier – about 230 AD – two different Christian writers describe it as Jesus' place of teaching. In that case, Bethpage was privileged indeed. Here the Son of God 'brought the true light of knowledge' as Jerome says. Here he came looking for the fruit of it – and found nothing.

He had already warned in a terrible parable what happens
to fig-trees that yield no fruit (Luke 13:6-9).

'Cut it down! Why should it use up the soil?' Now comes
the dread sentence: 'May no one ever eat fruit from you
again.' God's judgment, so often, is simply to say, 'Very well,
go the way of your own choice – be what you want to be',
with all the inevitable consequences of such a choice. 'The
essence of God's action in wrath is to *give men what they
choose*, in all its implications: nothing more and equally
nothing less.'[1] 'There are only two kinds of people in the
end: those who say to God, "Thy will be done", and those to
whom God says in the end, *thy* will be done. All that are in
Hell choose it.'[2]

Broken-hearted love confirms our determination to choose
our own way. Bethpage had made its choice, as Capernaum,
Bethsaida and Chorazin had made theirs.

Weeping over the city
The road down Olivet is steep – you lean backwards, your
sandals slapping on the hot stony path as you descend. Almost
always there are others making the same journey: chattering
tourists, serious pilgrims, earnest students. On Palm Sunday
1985 we joined the huge crowds that lined the entire route,
as an extraordinary variety of religious groups joined in the
traditional procession. Catholic nuns sang German hymns
and gently waved palm branches. Bearded priests swung
censers and intoned their prayers. Christian Zionists carried
banners proclaiming their love for Jerusalem. Some groups
of Arab Boy Scouts, flowing keffiyah over khaki uniforms,
hammered their drums and blew discordantly on their bugles.
British charismatics clapped and sang Spring Harvest songs
– 'Hosannah to the Son of David/Jesus the Messiah reigns'.

And – irony of ironies – Israeli soldiers stood impassively at vantage points, Uzi sub-machine guns at the ready, eyes flickering over the crowds. An army of occupation in Arab Jerusalem? An army of liberation in Zion? Forefront of American Christian Fundamentalism? Foretaste of the Redemption of Jerusalem? Scourge of the PLO and foe of the legitimate aspiration of Palestinians? The whole complex, contradictory confusion of modern Middle Eastern politics and religion was present that day, as it had been in the spring of 28 AD when Jesus the carpenter-rabbi rode in.

'As he approached Jerusalem and saw the city, he wept over it and said, "If you, even you, had only known this day what would bring you peace – but now it is hidden from your eyes"' (Luke 19:41-42).

This was no stiff upper-lip Westerner. Jesus was a man who lifted up his voice and wailed, the tears coursing his face. He knew. He anticipated the choice that would be made. 'Jesus Barabbas', the man of violence, guerilla leader and freedom fighter, spokesman for the oft-repeated view that men can liberate themselves by violence; that truth and justice grow out of the barrel of a gun; that the bomb is more effective than the ballot. And 'Jesus Bar-Joseph', the Prince of Peace, whose soldiers would have fought for him if his kingdom were that kind of kingdom, but it wasn't (John 18:36).

And, of course, he could see the consequence. They chose Barabbas, and the way of holy war. It was a choice which they kept on repeating for the next forty years. Until an exasperated Rome decided to settle the issue once and for all. Titus and Vespasian, son and father, general and future emperor, brought their armies to Jerusalem.

Jesus had warned, 'The days will come upon you when your enemies will build an embankment against you and

encircle you and hem you in on every side' (Luke 19:43). So
they did. Josephus, once defender of Galilee against the
Romans but now the invaders' war-correspondent, describes
the scene: 'Titus was now on the march from Caesarea. He
led three legions.... He ordered the fifth to join him via the
Emmaus route and the tenth to ascend by way of Jericho'.[3]

The grim silent encirclement of the city began. The fifth
legion made its base camp by Herod's family tomb (the
garden of the present King David Hotel) and facing Herod's
Palace (now the Jaffa Gate). Titus' famous tenth legion
camped on the slopes of Scopus-Olivet, just to the north of
where Jesus had stood and wept. The inexorable construction
of a siege-dyke began, just as Jesus had said.

The Christian Jews within the city knew what to do. Their
Master had spelled it out. 'When you see Jerusalem
surrounded by armies, you will know that its desolation is
near. Then let those who are in Judaea flee to the mountains,
let those in the city get out... for this is the time of punishment
in fulfilment of all that has been written' (Luke 21:20-22).
Led by their bishop, the Christians did exactly that – taking
refuge in Pella, across Jordan in Gentile Decapolis.

The siege which followed is described in stark realism
by Josephus. The pitiable tale is unique in literature for its
horrific detail. Attack and counter-attack dragged on, the
hopeless inhabitants fighting each other for food, staving off
one relentless attack after another, and watching horrified
from the walls as prisoners and deserters were crucified
around the perimeter by their captors.

> Many, as they buried the fallen, fell dead themselves... no weeping
> or lamentation was heard: hunger stifled emotion; and with dry eyes
> and grinning mouths those who were slow to die watched those
> whose death came sooner. Bodies at first were buried, for the stench

was intolerable; later, when this proved impossible, they flung them from the ramparts into the ravines.[4]

The inevitable end came. Section by section areas of the city fell to the legions. Titus ordered that the Temple itself should be preserved, and actually made various suggestions to the defenders as to how this could be ensured. A fascinating situation, this, for Jesus had said forty-two years earlier, that it would fall, and now the might of Rome, even as they capture it, says it shall stand.

> Some of his disciples were remarking about how the temple was adorned with beautiful stones and with gifts dedicated to God. But Jesus said, 'As for what you see here, the time will come when not one stone will be left on another; every one of them will be thrown down... when you see Jerusalem surrounded by armies you will know...' (Luke 21:5-6, 20-21).

So the prophet from Nazareth. Titus from Rome, backed by a superpower and awesome force said otherwise.

> I call on my army, on the Jews in my camp, and on you yourselves as witnesses that I am not compelling you to desecrate your Temple. If you change the battleground, no Roman will go near the holy places or violate them. I will protect the Temple for you even if you do not wish me to.[5]

Who would be proved correct? The man on the donkey or the man in the tank?

> Titus returned to the Antonia, intending to launch a full-scale attack the following day at dawn and take possession of the Temple. The sanctuary, however, had long before been condemned by God to the flames.... One of the soldiers, urged on by some supernatural force, snatched a blazing piece of wood and, climbing on another soldier's back, hurled the flaming brand through a low golden window.[6]

A messenger brought the news to Titus, who dashed to the scene followed by senior officers, and tried to bring events under control.

> But his shouts were not heard and his beckoning hands went unheeded amid the avenging fury. No exhortation or threat could now restrain the impetuosity of the legions for passion was in supreme command.
>
> Pretending not even to hear Caesar's orders, they threw in more firebrands... carnage spread... the heap of corpses mounted higher and higher about the altar, a stream of blood flowed down the Temple's steps, and the bodies of those slain at the top slipped to the bottom.
>
> While the Temple was ablaze, the attackers plundered it, and countless people were slaughtered. Such was the height of the hill and the magnitude of the blazing pile that the entire city seemed to be ablaze. The Temple Mount, everywhere enveloped in flames, seemed to be boiling over from its base; yet the blood seemed more abundant than the flames. The ground could not be seen between the corpses; the soldiers climbed over heaps of bodies.[7]

The awful events of 70 AD left a scar on the racial consciousness of the Jew. It was the end of their nation. For nineteen centuries 'the wandering Jew' had been an enigma of history, scattered throughout the world, different yet indefinable – and then, unthinkably, in the twentieth century, coming back to his land and his city, impelled by the events of two world wars, the collapse of empires, the horrors of the holocaust that multiplied sixfold the terrible scenes described by Josephus.

I slipped Bible and Josephus back into my knapsack and took a spectacular photograph of the Kedron valley below the city walls. Holding hands to steady each other, we continued our scrambling descent.

On our left, behind a low wall, long lines of gravestones

THE DONKEY AND THE TANK

marked a modern cemetery. A little group of *hassidim* clustered around a new grave, rocking and swaying as they chattered their prayers, each laying a little stone on the large slab, to mark their pious visit. I recalled learning at the university that two hundred tombstones had been discovered dating back to the time of Jesus. Is that what he could have meant?

'Some of the Pharisees in the crowd said to Jesus, "Teacher, rebuke your disciples!"

"I tell you," he replied, "if they keep quiet, the stones will cry out"' (Luke 19:39-40).

A magnificent piece of oriental hyperbole? Or did he mean exactly that? 'Keep my disciples quiet on this day of proclamation, and these very tombstones will crack open, as those who have gone before me bear witness from their graves that I am king, and will soon be conqueror of death.' Not so wild as it sounds at first, for something like that happened a few days later.

> When Jesus had cried out again in a loud voice, he gave up his spirit.... The tombs broke open and the bodies of many holy people who had died were raised to life. They came out of the tombs, and after Jesus' resurrection they went into the holy city and appeared to many people (Matt. 27:50-53).

We met Bishop John as we reached the last turn in the path before Gethsemane. The Mount of Olives is part of his diocese. I had come to know him well, in his dark blue robe and little fez-like hat, his ginger beard as incongruous as ever. For this bishop of the ancient Church of the East, now mainly Arab, but tracing unbroken physical descent from the early disciples in Galilee, is a Scotsman! A very fine scholar, too. We paused and discussed for a few moments the subject

that is uppermost in every walk on Olivet – the Kingship of
Christ.

He shared a few details of a debate he'd recently had
with Jewish rabbis. Reading of the Talmud and other
rabbinical sources had led him to suspect that a strand of
ancient Jewish thinking spoke in terms of the *torah* (the Law
of God) as *personal* – very much as the Book of Proverbs
speaks of *wisdom*. This the rabbis admitted, and together
they plunged into the prologue to John's Gospel where Jesus
is declared as the *Word*, present with God at the moment of
creation, co-equal with God, yet distinct from him, and 'The
Word became flesh and lived for a while among us. We have
seen his glory... full of grace and truth' (John 1:14).

In the time of Jesus, a raised arched road, simply called
'the way', spanned the lower slope of Olivet across to the
rising ground beyond the Kedron stream. It led straight into
the Golden Gate, and thence to the Temple courtyard in direct
line with the great altar. Presumably Christ rode this way:
'Jesus entered Jerusalem and went to the temple. He looked
around at everything, but since it was already late, he went
out to Bethany with the Twelve' (Mark 11:11).

Matthew and Luke telescope the next day's events and
make them appear at first sight to be the climax of the
'triumphal entry'. But Mark is quite specific. The 'cleansing
of the temple' was no unpremeditated event, performed in
the excitement of a popular demonstration, rendering disorder
and military intervention inevitable. Jesus looked around,
confirmed what previous visits had already suggested, left
by the southern staircase, and laid his plans for the next day.
At this point he was fulfilling Zechariah's vision, not
Malachi's; the lowly king riding on a donkey, rather than the
Lord suddenly appearing in his temple to purge it.

But Ezekiel's enigmatic prophecy, too, found its consummation and deepest meaning now. The present Golden Gate is only 500 years old. Below it, beneath the present soil-level, lies the gate Jesus used. The present gate is a curious place, for it is totally blocked with carefully shaped stones, apparently put there not long after its construction. Why? Tales and legends abound, passed on by Jews, Christians and Muslims. It is Arab property, and part of their 'holy place'. Visitors may walk within 200 yards of the inside of it, on the 'temple mount', but go any nearer and you will be hustled away with gestures, scowls and much flapping of sleeves and scowling. With elaborate unconcern Rita wandered closer whilst I kept several people engaged in conversation – and took a much-prized picture.

Looking at that blocked gate, a memory stirred, but a concordance was not available. Later at the house, I checked. Yes – how odd. Ezekiel. First of all that picture from chapter 43.

'Then the man brought me *to the gate facing east*, and I saw the glory of the God of Israel coming *from the east*... The glory of the LORD entered the temple through *the gate facing east*' (verses 1-4).

Well, that fitted Palm Sunday, in a strange, unlooked-for way. But what about the gate being blocked? Yes, here it is in the next chapter.

Then the man brought me back to the outer gate of the sanctuary, the one facing east, and it was shut. The LORD said to me, 'This gate is to remain shut. It must not be opened; no-one may enter through it. It is to remain shut because the LORD, the God of Israel, has entered through it. The prince himself is the only one who may sit inside the gateway...' (Ezek. 44:1-3).

Bible prophecy is a strange thing. So often its import and intention is not clear until the fulfilment comes. A donkey tethered to a vine, a king lowly on an ass, the glory of God coming through the temple gateway: Jesus and his disciples, amidst shouted songs and waving palm branches.

Of course *this* one is not the actual gate of Jesus' time. I talked to someone who had spent years studying on the spot. He showed me a remarkable photograph. With permission, he had dug one dark night outside and in front of the gate. Soon he reached the curved lintel of the original structure, and then the space within the ancient gateway came into view. This too was blocked up, not only with stones, but with human bones!

Two explanations were given to him. One quoted Muslim writings (Suna 79:14) in which the gate is the symbolic entrance to heaven, and therefore a suitable place to bury people. Another Arab authority gave a more elaborate explanation. Muslims reluctantly concede that a Jewish messiah-figure may come, whom they assume will be a priest. But in the Old Testament, no priest can cross or touch a human body without becoming ceremonially unclean. So, if you pack the gate with bones the Messiah can never enter! Is it as easy as that? I have news. It will take more than bones to keep out the King of Kings!

Our walk was over. Palm Sunday had ended with a demonstration by uniformed Arabs marching the city boundaries with blaring bands and thrumming drums. They were making a religious and political point. As Christians, they were adding another twist to the kaleidoscope of Middle Eastern politics, and making another appeal to the figure of Jesus for support. Who was this man on a donkey, and why is it that his name is so often invoked in the cause of the tank?

Will the real Jesus stand up?

The name of the man from Nazareth occupies a curious place in Israel today. Muslims affect to admire him – but strictly as a prophet, with no divine sonship, no saving cross, no resurrection. Mormons have built a huge university in his name on that very Mount of Olives. But what Mormons say about Jesus is an extraordinary mix of Christianity, polytheism and occultism, with a smooth surface overlay of biblical phraseology. Jehovah's Witnesses come to Jerusalem in large numbers, and tramp around the Garden of the Tomb. They acknowledge him as some kind of king and speak much of his kingdom – yet empty his cross of its vital meaning and deny the physical reality of his rising from the grave. Priests of ancient oriental churches chant his name in prolonged ceremonies that emphasise his remoteness and difference and seem to divorce him almost totally from everyday human life. And Jews – what do they think?

Amongst Israelis, Jesus is a frequent talking-point. As a Christian spending a summer term in the Hebrew University, I conversed with Jewish students about Jesus almost every day, usually at their request. There was no need to force him into the conversation, for he is a talking point.

For most, the old attitude to 'That One' (name never spoken, in distaste and anger) has long since gone. The Jewishness of Jesus has been rediscovered by Jew and Gentile alike. Some see him as a Zealot leader, an apocalyptic prophet and freedom fighter. This can only be proposed by making a nonsense of our primary sources of information; the Gospel records. The man on the donkey simply cannot be turned into the driver of the tank, even by tongue-in-cheek pop-religious writers like Schonfield with his 'Passover Plot'.

Others see him as radical rabbi, in the tradition of Pharisaism at its best. There is some truth in this, but only a partial truth. The writings of Geza Vermes have contributed a great deal to Jewish appreciation of Jesus at the scholarly level.[8] More recently the Jerusalem School of Synoptic Studies (Jews and Christians researching together) have furthered the process.[9]

The Dead Sea Scrolls are often appealed to by well-meaning Israeli guides as the key to understanding Jesus. But in spite of some overlap of language and thought (inevitable when the same subject is being addressed in the same time and place), Jesus would have been given short shrift by the Essene Community. They regarded the strictest Pharisees as easy-going libertines: what would they have made of the friend of publicans and sinners?

Joseph, an Israeli guide, had taken my friends around the country for eight days, and was visibly impressed by their joyful and simple faith (many were new Christians). He watched, round-eyed, as I served communion to them at the Garden Tomb. Next day, exploring Emmaus, I read that lovely story once more of the two disciples who invited the stranger to their Emmaus home and only discovered it was the risen Christ when he said grace with the simple meal. I had brought some long Arab loaves, the crust sprinkled with sesame seed. We broke them into meal-sized chunks and ate them in a circle, then held hands and sang, 'He is Lord, He is risen from the dead and He is Lord.'

I beckoned to our Israeli friend. 'This is not communion – simply eating in friendship,' I said. 'Please join us as our friend.' He did so, deeply affected and in tears. 'May I say something?' he asked. 'Not as your professional guide, but as Joseph, your friend. You are beautiful people, and I have

experienced your love. You say the Messiah has come. I say
he is still to come. If, one day, he comes, and he turns out to
be Jesus, then I shall not be surprised, and all of us will be
glad.'

Of course that won't quite do. But it does illustrate a
changing attitude to Jesus and to genuine Christians. Marco
was a middle-aged student at the University, over from
America for the summer. He and his wife asked me to guide
them along the Via Dolorosa, to which an archaeology lecture
had made passing reference. We finished at the Garden Tomb,
and they stood pensively inside in the dim coolness. 'You
know, I could go for most of what you say about Jesus,'
Marco remarked. The King still rides into people's lives in
Jerusalem today, and demands a response.

An Israeli in his twenties listened to me preaching on the
kingship of Christ in a local church, and asked to talk to me
afterwards. 'I believe everything you say,' he commented. 'I
had lost my faith in God. Atheism left me empty and
frustrated. One day, sitting in a Jerusalem garden, I actually
saw Jesus and knew he was the Messiah.'

I stared at him. 'You mean saw with your physical eyes?'

'Yes.'

'Do you mind me asking what he looked like?'

'Well – strange – I can only say he was ordinary height
but at the same time looked ten feet tall.'

'How did you know he was Jesus? Did he *tell* you he
was the Messiah?'

'No – it was like in a dream – you just kind of know
without being told.'

'Did the vision – appearance – dream – whatever it was
– *convince* you?'

'No – I shook it off – even dabbled in Buddhism for a

time – but I could never forget it. Eventually I began to read
the Bible – my Old Testament and your New. I found some
Jews who believed in Jesus – and then, just like anyone
else, Jew or Gentile, I had to repent and believe and be
baptised.'

References
1. James Packer, *Knowing God*, Hodder & Stoughton, 1973, p. 139.
2. C. S. Lewis, *The Great Divorce*, Collins Foundation Books, 1977, chapter 9, pp. 66-67.
3. Josephus, *The Jewish War*, Bk V, chapter 1, para 6:40-42, pp. 321-322.
4. Josephus, *ibid*, Bk V, chapter 12, para 3:514-518, p. 395.
5. Josephus, *ibid*, Bk VI, chapter 2, para 4:128, p. 410.
6. Josephus, *ibid*, Bk VI, chapter 4, para 5: 249-252, p. 421.
7. Josephus, *ibid*, Bk VI, chapter 5, para 1:271-277, p. 423.
8. Geza Vermes, *Jesus the Jew – A Historian's Reading of the Gospels* (1973); *The Gospel of Jesus the Jew* (1981); *Jesus and the World of Judaism* (1983) all SCM Press.
9. The Jerusalem School of Synoptic Research, as it is now called, was pioneered by the late Dr. Robert Lindsey, minister of Narkis Street Baptist Church in West Jerusalem, and the Israeli scholar, Professor David Flusser. Their quarterly high-quality journal *Jerusalem Perspective* can be obtained from PO Box 31820, 9137 Jerusalem, Israel.

Part Four

The Saviour

In the experience of reconciliation to God through Christ is to be found the principle and the touchstone of all genuine Christian doctrine. Whatever can be derived from it is true and necessary; whatever is incompatible with it lacks the essential Christian character (James Denney).

'Are you thirsty?' said the Lion.

'I'm *dying* of thirst,' said Jill.

'Then drink,' said the Lion.

'May I – could I – would you mind going away while I do?' said Jill.

The Lion answered this only by a look and a very low growl...

'I daren't come and drink,' said Jill.

'Then you will die of thirst,' said the Lion.

'Oh dear!' said Jill, coming another step nearer. 'I suppose I must go and look for another stream then.'

'There is no other stream,' said the Lion.

(C S Lewis, *The Silver Chair*, chapter 2)

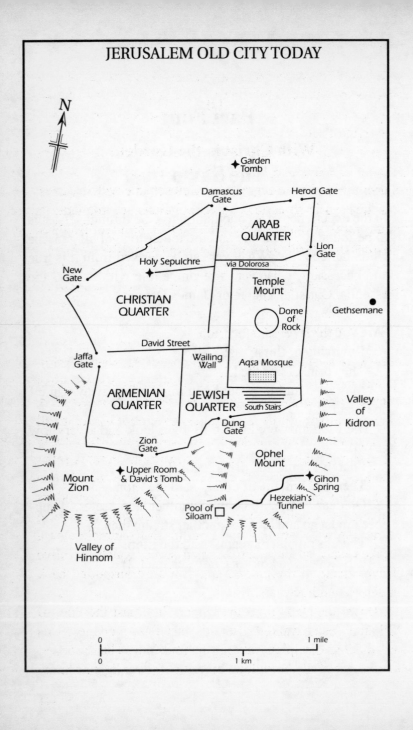

JERUSALEM OLD CITY TODAY

N

Garden Tomb

Damascus Gate

Herod Gate

ARAB QUARTER

Lion Gate

Holy Sepulchre

via Dolorosa

New Gate

Temple Mount

Dome of Rock

Gethsemane

CHRISTIAN QUARTER

David Street

Jaffa Gate

Wailing Wall

Aqsa Mosque

ARMENIAN QUARTER

JEWISH QUARTER

South Stairs

Valley of Kidron

Zion Gate

Dung Gate

Upper Room & David's Tomb

Ophel Mount

Gihon Spring

Mount Zion

Pool of Siloam

Hezekiah's Tunnel

Valley of Hinnom

0   1 mile

0   1 km

10

With Christ in the Garden

I don't think I have ever visited Gethsemane with dry eyes. Its location is so certain, its associations so poignant, its appearance so suggestive. Childhood memories of Brethren hymns merge with pictures from illustrated Bibles.

> Gethsemane, can I forget?
> Or there thy conflict see,
> Thine agony and blood-like sweat,
> And not remember Thee?

The word 'Gethsemane' (more correctly, Gat-shemen) simply means oil-press. The whole area of the lower Olivet slopes was planted with olive-groves (as the name suggests), and where graveyards or churches have left it alone, it still is. The winter stream of Kidron (as Luke wholly accurately describes it) only runs after the winter rains, but it is sufficient to provide the valley floor with moisture and silt, and make hardy olives even more fruitful than usual. Nowadays the stream is tidily culverted, and a busy road crosses it, humming with Jericho-bound traffic. But scramble over a broken wall, sit on a sun-warmed stone, watch the olive leaves rustle in the breeze, and you are transported back nineteen hundred years.

Down the steps from the Upper City, past the Pool of Siloam, Jesus walked after his last Passover meal, his bewildered disciples trudging behind him. The moon, of course, was full; the valley a mixture of silver light and inky shadows. Passover 1985 coincided with Good Friday, so the traditional Thursday Walk of Christians had extra significance. The various Christian congregations take a three hour walk, starting at half-hour intervals, from a communion service at the Upper Room, down through the cobbled lanes, across Kidron and into Gethsemane, stopping to read the biblical accounts and sing a hymn at appropriate spots. Down in the deep valley we could look up and see clusters of torches as later groups zig-zagged down the slope. Snatches of their songs carried to us. 'Ride on, ride on in majesty'; 'Lest I forget Gethsemane'; 'In the cross of Christ I glory'; 'Thank you, Jesus, thank you, Lord, for loving me'...

The route took us (as it took Jesus) past the King's Garden where Solomon piped water from Gihon Spring; trees and flowers still grow in extra profusion. He wrote his Song of Songs here, and we paused to recall those evocative words in the light of the simple, sacred fellowship meal we had just shared. 'He brought me to his banquet hall, and his banner over me is love' (Song of Solomon 2:4).

A tomb loomed up on our right; it was there when Jesus passed, for it is dated. Here, too, stands Absalom's monument (rebuilt in Jesus' time). Jewish fathers used to bring their children here, tell them the story of David's spoilt and wayward son – and give them a walloping to reinforce the need for obedience! What were the thoughts of 'great David's greater Son' who, in total obedience to his Father's will, was soon to face agony and darkness? Zechariah's monument also stood then as it still stands today by the Kidron path. Was Jesus passing this spot when he quoted from that prophet? 'I will strike the shepherd and the sheep will be scattered' (Mark 14:26-27, quoting Zech. 13:7).

Can we really kneel where Jesus knelt in the garden that

will forever be associated with his 'obedience unto death'?
The whole lower slope of Olivet on its western (Jerusalem)
side can fairly bear the name. The Gospel writers are more
specific. There was an *enclosed orchard* across Kidron. Judas knew the place because Jesus often retired there with
his disciples (John 18:1-2). To Luke, too, it was 'the usual
place' (Luke 22:39-40). Jesus paused three times in the area,
first to leave eight of his disciples 'sitting here' (Mark 14:32),
second leaving Peter, James and John 'over there' (Matt.
26:36-37), and finally moving on himself 'a stone's throw
beyond them' (Luke 22:40-41). The eye-witness memories
come through powerfully.

The name Gethsemane has never gone out of use from
then until now. And curiously enough, there are *three* spots
preserved separately for denominational reasons, which
could very easily correspond to the movement of events. A
little cave called Gethsemane Grotto has a domed roof, a
skylight through to the sloping garden above, and artificial
cisterns, channels and rock-hewn bowls which indicate an
oil-press. It is old enough to have given the name originally
to the area. Later it became a Christian meeting place with
stone benches ('sit here'!) and later again a Christian burial-
place. Now silent brown-robed Franciscans keep it as a simple chapel.

I sat and considered, one August morning. A visit to a
younger and better-preserved oil-press nearer Bethany had
already given me the clues. Olives were a staple food in
Jesus' time. For Arabs, they still are. They provide nutritious food, fuel for the lamps, and oil as a sovereign remedy
for many medical ailments. Life, light and healing. *But first
the olives must be crushed.* A huge millstone breaks them
into a mush, after which the thick liquid is poured into a

bowl and a great wooden screw with a flat disc is turned
into it until the pure oil runs. Broken, crushed and pressed
that we might have life and light and healing. So it was with
the Son of God as he faced the ultimate horror of his suffering for our sins – 'And being in anguish he prayed more
earnestly, and his sweat was like drops of blood falling to
the ground' (Luke 22:44).

I was remembering in my prayers a relative of mine, an
older man, who that day was burying his wife in far-off England. I wrote a letter before I left the cave: 'As you grieve at
the funeral, I am praying for you in a place called Gethsemane. As you probably know, Jesus here faced the darkness
that awaited him. Because he went into it alone, we need
never be alone. I pray that you will discover the comfort of
that fact.' He treasured the letter, and showed me it, back in
England shortly before *he* died, and bore quiet witness to
his own readiness.

Slightly below the cave and nearer the stream, the massive Church of All Nations stands, with its great multicoloured frontage facing the Eastern Gate of the city. Otherwise
known as the Basilica of the Agony, it stands where earlier
Crusader and Byzantine chapels stood. Pushing through its
floor is an area of unlevelled rock which, at least since 380
AD, has been marked by Christians as the place where Jesus
knelt alone. Immediately behind it a quiet garden, divided
into two enclosed areas by Roman Catholic and Russian
Orthodox, marks the third spot, and embodies the garden
which the imaginative Bible-reader has always envisaged.
There, on Passover eve, several hundred of us knelt in the
moonlight and thanked him who was obedient unto death for
our salvation.

Innocence on trial

In poignant words, Peter, who witnessed some of it, described the unforgettable mien of the suffering King as he moved from Gethsemane via Caiaphas's palace to Pilate's judgment hall: 'When they hurled their insults at him, he did not retaliate; when he suffered he made no threats. Instead, he entrusted himself to him who judges justly' (1 Pet. 2:23).

The best way to understand the 'trial' of Jesus is to grasp what it should have been and then in contrast see what it was. The Mishnah gives the ideal of Jewish justice. The Sanhedrin (Great Council) was the supreme court. 'Mercy in Judgment' was its motto. They took the attitude that the prisoner is almost always right. Not only was he innocent until proven guilty, but he was not even on trial until all the evidence of witnesses had been given, sifted and proved. It must have been an ordeal to give evidence at all; the witness must be of good character, the details of his evidence meticulously correct and in total agreement with other witnesses whose evidence he could not listen to. In a case with possible death sentence, a night for prayer and consideration must intervene between evidence and sentence. No part of the trial could be held at night, or before the Sabbath, or before a religious festival. Finally, the prisoner must not have put to him a direct question from which he might incriminate himself, and no prisoner could be found guilty on the basis of his own replies alone.

Follow Jesus' actual ordeal, and you can now see how outrageously Caiaphas and his squalid crew broke every canon of legality and justice. They represented one small power-group within the nation. How inaccurate it is to say 'the Jews (all of them ?) crucified Jesus'.

Before Annas (John 18:13-14)

Annas had been sacked from the high priesthood by the Romans, but his own family (four successive sons) intrigued successfully for the job, and the position at that moment was occupied by his son-in-law. Annas was still the power behind the throne. A Roman saying refers to his family's nepotism as 'Coming and going like flies on a sore'. There was a local Jewish saying: 'the sons of Annas take the high priesthood, make their sons priests, their nephews temple treasurers, and their servants beaters of the people.' Annas of course, already had a score to settle with Jesus: his 'bazaar' had taken a rude shaking a few days before at the hands of this young reformer. This interview presumably happened in his private residence, or at his son-in-law's official palace. We have no details of what ensued. Perhaps the old man simply had a gloating look at the prisoner.

Before Caiaphas (John 18:19-23)

This encounter certainly happened at the palace. It seems to have been a kind of preliminary investigation. The high priest tried to get some facts out of Jesus 'about his disciples and his preaching'. The whole proceeding was illegal (at night, before a Sabbath, before any witnesses had spoken, and putting direct questions to the prisoner). Jesus pointed this out with quiet dignity, and took a beating for doing so.

Where in fact *was* the palace? Two possible sites are offered today. One, a stopping-place for religious processions to remember the event, is based on old religious tradition established for purely liturgical reasons (as is the whole of the Via Dolorosa, at the far side of the city). The other, excavated by Franciscans early this century, has suggestive though not conclusive archaeological facts in its favour. Visually it is stunning, and my first visit to it was a profound experience.

We clambered up Maccabean and Roman steps from the Kidron valley. It is practically certain that Jesus descended them on his night walk from the Upper Room to Gethsemane, and was hurried up them by guards who arrested him. Inscriptions include the word *corban* (Mark 7:11). Special temple balance-weights found here all date from Caiaphas's time. The three-layered ruin stands on a steep slope, with a courtyard slightly below the entrance, and dungeons below the courtyard. One of the guides, employed by the Catholic church perched on the ruins, seemed to be an American charismatic. With quiet conviction she retold the story, and we realised that we were standing by the charcoal fire with Peter, looking up to the doorway as Jesus appeared. 'The Lord turned and looked straight at Peter. Then Peter remembered... and went outside and wept bitterly' (Luke 22:61-62).

How easy was Peter's swift change from 'I shan't deny you even if the others do' to 'I never knew the man'. His volatile character and his tendency to speak first and think later no doubt played a part. He would have been totally bewildered also by Jesus' own attitude – inviting arrest and discouraging resistance. There is subtle psychology at work here too. Peter was braced to meet plotting priests and brutal guards; what he tripped over was a servant-girl who casually, perhaps jokingly, said something like, 'You're not one of *his* lot, are you!' The Greek sentence implies a negative: she expected the answer, 'No, not likely!' It is the *unexpected* in temptation that so easily stumbles us: Peter is committed to irreversible denial almost before he has thought about it.

The guide took us down to the dungeons: grim, cold, si-

lent. A whipping-post stands, gaunt and hideous. The victim's arms were tied to rings in the T-shaped pillar. Little
basins scooped out of the rock at his feet would have held
saltwater and oil to sprinkle on the hideous lacerations in a
belated touch of medical treatment afterwards. Jesus was
not in fact scourged here – that was later, in the Roman
praetorium. Here, Peter and John must have been tortured on
a later occasion when the Sanhedrin tried to shut them up
(Acts 5:40-41). But as they awaited their flogging, they could
well have crouched in the same cell where Jesus waited
whilst priestly father and son-in-law conferred and the Sanhedrin gathered.

Two of the women in our party stopped at the head of the
winding stairs and burst into tears. With great sensitivity the
guide murmured to me, 'Do try to persuade them to come
down. They are women with personal sorrows. Let them
stand where he who bore their sorrows stood. They'll cry it
out in his presence, and be better for it.' She was right. One
had been recently widowed in young middle-age. The other
was grieving over a broken marriage. From that day onwards
there was a quiet serenity in the way they began to cope.

I've stood there often since, and never failed to sense the
nearness of the Man of Sorrows. Another guide on one occasion, a little Armenian, quietly spoke of 'my Saviour' with
tears running down his wizened cheeks. My own voice wob-
bled as, at his request, I read a few words of Scripture. He
murmured to me, 'You know him too – I can tell.' The tourists that time were not confessing Christians. One of them, a
big American with a stetson, said, 'Thank you for the way
you read that. There was something special... I don't know...'
and he walked away, shaking his head.

St Peter in Gallicantu (Latin for cockcrow) is a particularly beautiful church through which the visitor has to walk to reach the dungeons. The odd, eerie feeling of passing rapidly through different layers of history is particularly acute here. Jewish Nazarenes; Byzantine Christians, Crusader knights from medieval England and Germany, French Franciscans in the nineteenth century – all have worshipped here, all have pondered on Jesus' suffering and Peter's penitence.

Before the Sanhedrin (Mark 14:55-65)

First light would be about 4.30 a.m. There must have been some hasty messages sent across the city as day dawned, and the next stage of the trial began. The Sanhedrin required a quorum of twenty-three members. Awkward members like Nicodemus and Joseph could have been left out. Recent excavations have uncovered a stone inscription at the foot of the southern staircase of the temple. It bears the word *zekinim* ('elders', Matt. 27:4). This confirms the statement of the Mishnah, which describes them meeting in the Hall of Hewn Stone, somewhere in the temple precincts.

The members would sit in a semi-circle, so that each could see the reaction of the others. The case should have begun with arguments for the defence: here there were none. Every canon of legality was outraged, the 'witnesses' disagreed, and Jesus was misquoted in a manner which could have no bearing on a capital charge.

The high priest committed the final outrage: a direct incriminating question, which was forbidden.

Jesus' answer is often misunderstood. It was not a prophecy of his second coming. Rather, it was a direct, deliberate claim to be the fulfilment of that divine promise which above all others had given current shape to the Messianic hope. He quoted *verbatim* Daniel 7:13-14: not Messiah on earth, but

Messiah before the throne of God is pictured there. Jesus
says in effect, 'At the moment I stand before you. One day
you will kneel before me.'

Before Pilate (John 18:28-19:16)
The Sanhedrin now had the vestige of a charge against him,
even if illegally reached: a false claim to Messiahship (as
they saw it) could be construed as blasphemy. But they now
had a new problem. In 30 AD the Roman authority had removed the Sanhedrin's right to hand down a death sentence.
Pilate, the procurator, must do that. So, changing the charge
from a religious to a political one, they hurried Jesus to the
'palace of the Roman governor' as John calls it.

Where was this? Probably in the hated Antonia Fortress,
built into the north-west corner of the Temple area. Here a
Roman garrison kept order in the city. The procurator, normally resident in cooler seaside Caesarea, moved to the capital with reinforcements during the excitable and dangerous
festivals. Some recent scholars have located Pilate's part-
time residence in the palace of Herod the Great, over the
western edge of the city (today's Jaffa Gate). Even more
recently archaeologists like Dan Bahat have proposed yet
another site, south-west of the Temple and somewhere under the new restored Jewish Quarter. The Antonia Fortress
still seems most likely to me. Its site is easily traceable, the
once great four-towered building now replaced by an Arab
school, two ancient churches and a convent. You can still
see the two remaining steps of the flight that led down from
the barracks into the Temple courtyards. A squad of soldiers
at the double could be there in minutes when the perennial
'troubles' broke out in the shrine. That's what happened when
the apostle Paul found himself almost lynched in a near-riot

(Acts 21:27-36). He then persuaded the officer in charge to let him make a defence from here as he 'stood on the steps, motioned to the crowd, and when all were silent, began to speak' (verse 40). An eye-witness memory if ever there was one! By a curious coincidence, the controversial new exit from the 'Hasmonean Tunnel' emerges into the Via Dolorosa at this point.

Pilate was in a sticky position. Secular history throws a flood of light on his hesitations, posturing and changeability as Jesus stood before him. Three times already his mishandling of the Jewish authorities and the mob had landed him in trouble and forced him to back off from confrontation. Once he had tried to pillage Temple funds to build an aqueduct. Once he forced pagan military insignia into the Temple area but had to withdraw them again. Each incident focuses on Pilate's tendency to try to condescend to local prejudices whilst insisting on Roman authority.

Now the priests really put the screws on. 'If you let this man go, you are no friend of Caesar. Anyone who claims to be a king opposes Caesar' (John 19:12). Pilate was trapped in the tangled web of his own earlier cruelties and mismanagements.

The whole dramatic scene was played out in front of 'the judge's seat at a place known as the Stone Pavement, which in Aramaic is Gabbatha', John tells us (19:13). We must imagine a raised dais, Roman-paved, with a portico behind, on which Pilate engaged in his extraordinary private consultations with Jesus in between public appearances to argue with the priests and the gathering mob. Guides today will show you 'Pilate's Arch', half across the narrow lane of the Via Dolorosa, and half inside the church beside the lane. Unfortunately, although the site may be correct this cannot

be Gabbatha itself, for it is now evident that the arch was
built a hundred years later by Hadrian, as a triumphal arch.
But the church's name *Ecce Homo* (Behold the man) vividly
recreates the scene as the mockery of a trial, interrupted by a
brief and futile excursion to Herod's residence, comes to its
terrible end.

It may have happened within yards of here. Knock on the
door of the Convent of the Sisters of Zion, as I often have
done at night, feeling like Peter persuading Rhoda to let him
in (Acts 12:12-14) – and for the same reason – to attend a
prayer meeting of the Jerusalem believers. You will be welcomed by gentle-voiced nuns who will show you Roman
paving-stones that could well be the very place where yawn-
ing soldiers awaited the outcome of the trial, and vented
their anti-Semitism on Jesus the prisoner by crowning him
in mockery with a cap of twisted thorns. Some of the stones
bear marks of the king's game – a kind of chess board on
which soldiers used prisoners as the 'pawns', and mocked
the winner who remained on the king's square at the end of
the game. Did he stand here, patient in suffering? A monk lay
face-down on the stones, lost in prayer. People I recently
led to Christ knelt, awed, and touched the stones with their
fingertips. I read the story aloud, and found a lump in my
throat and tears in my eyes. We sang together,

> King of my life I crown thee now;
> Thine may the glory be!
> Lest I forget thy thorn-crowned brow,
> Lead me to Calvary.

The nun nodded gently. Our Israeli guide watched big-eyed.
What is it that moves these Christians to love this land, and
to insist that one of its rabbis is the Son of God – and their

loved friend? He commented later, 'I feel closer to the Lord through being with you and watching you.'

Who is really on trial?
The overwhelming impression of these far-off events is extraordinary. For through them all it is the prisoner who moves with the quiet dignity of conscious power. The judges are on trial. It is their malicious cruelties and miserable compromises that stand condemned, their malevolent misuse of power that has 'guilty' written all over it.

Consider. Jewish religion was, to say the least, the highest expression of pious human instinct. Roman justice was renowned for its fairness and competence. Confronted by the only sinless man the world has ever known, they (between them) betrayed every instinct, broke every rule, and savaged every compassionate feeling. Here were the 'principalities and powers', as the apostle Paul would later describe them. Originally part of God's creation, instruments of his will for order, they have tragically shared in mankind's fall, and been captured for Satan's purposes. And Jesus, in his steady progress to the cross, '...disarmed the powers and authorities (and) made a public spectacle of them, triumphing over them by the cross' (Col. 2:15).

So many typical expressions of power were present that long night and chill morning. The power of military might (Roman soldiers); the power of popular opinion (the morning mob at the Pavement); the power of religion (the Sadducees); the power of long tradition (the Pharisees); the power of political expediency (Pilate); the power of money (Judas); the power of personal fear (Peter) – all of them familiar from today's television news bulletins. In a very real sense, they drove Jesus to the cross. *But he won, and they lost.*[1]

Jesus has had the ultimate victory. The powers stand, self-condemned – as Hendrick Berkhof, fresh from Nazism's bloodstained downfall wrote: 'These are the Powers that dominate mankind and are accepted as ultimate realities. But at the crucifixion, their true nature became apparent. The weapon of illusion from which they derived their strength was struck out of their hands.'[2]

Redeeming love and suffering endured have released a power into the lives of millions that no dictator can enforce or destroy.

References

1. I discuss this at some length in my *Jesus, The Man and His Message*, Christian Focus Publications, 1995, chapter 8, 'The Man who Exposed the Powers'.
2. Hendrick Berkhof, *Christ and the Powers*, translated by John H Yoder, Herald Press, Ontario, 1962, p. 39.

11

Behold the Wondrous Cross

Enter the old city by the Jaffa Gate, as General Allenby did on a famous and oft-quoted occasion. Turn left as soon as possible, at right angles to the Arab shops and souks of David Street which bisects the city from west to east. Dive down some steps, and you are in a different world. The Christian Quarter of the old city welcomes you.

It is still very Arabic: it always comes as something of a shock to discover that Arabs may well be Christians. Bishop Kafiti, until recently Anglican Bishop in Jerusalem, felt sore about that. 'Christians come from Europe and America on pilgrimage and never meet an indigenous Christian, visit an Arab congregation, or show any awareness of the ancient church of the Middle East,' he complained to me once.

The fact is that 'Arab' members of the ancient Christian churches spoke the language of Jesus for centuries, until forced by Islamic occupation to become Arabic speaking.

A few twists and turns, and you are outside the Church of the Holy Sepulchre. Here is the central shrine of Christendom. A millennium ago it was to Crusaders what the golden fleece was to Jason and the holy grail to King Arthur's knights. The vast, dark, rambling, echoing edifice leaves many modern Christians uneasy, bewildered and disillusioned. The first time I accidentally wandered in, I fled within minutes. A greasy character, some lower order of ecclesiastic, approached me with the mien of an Egyptian selling doubtful postcards. For so many shekels, he whispered, he would – what? I wasn't sure, and did not wait to find out.

A bearded face peered out from a parted curtain covering some crevice in the wall, and offered me a candle, at a price. The sharp sickly smell of incense filled the porticoed gloom and a dolorous chanting echoed through the smoke. Clanking chains suitable to adorn skeletons in dungeons festooned the ceilings with swinging censers. Crucifixes adorned with gold and precious stones hung in the flickering light of candles by the score. That was enough; I hurried back into the sunlight.

Since then, I've dutifully forced myself to return to this morbid shrine and explore the convoluted history which it enshrines. Here, without doubt, great events have happened, great piety has been displayed, and great lunacies have been perpetrated. People have walked for a year to reach its porches and kiss its stones. The Crusaders marched here to set the blood of Arabs and Jews running ankle-deep in the lanes around, and to reclaim it in triumph for the Prince of Peace.

But did Jesus really die and rise again in the general area of these vast rambling halls? Certainly Christians for fifteen hundred years have thought so. One's first reaction is, 'This can't be the place!'. Examination of the evidence brings me to 'I hope it isn't.' Further examination of the evidence drives one to the reluctant conclusion that it may well be. Rational thought is difficult here. Some guides, professionally sensitive to their clients' likely reaction, avoid the place altogether if they are with Protestants. That is a mistake. By any standards, here is one of the most extraordinary, atmospheric and controversial buildings on this globe. And I do know people who have encountered Christ in these echoing vaults.

A piece of detection
Putting together the alleged evidence is a confusing business. Tantalising hints abound. False clues clamour. One thing

is clear. When Constantine became the first Christian Roman Emperor, his mother Helena visited the Holy Land in search of places of which it could be said, 'Here it happened'. The Mount of Olives was no problem, and Bethlehem provided few puzzles, but Jerusalem had been completely levelled and rebuilt by Hadrian a hundred years after the foundation of the Church and almost two hundred years before Helena arrived. Whatever she found, whatever reasoning she pursued, within a short while she had the emperor's funds and a site for the erection of a lavish building to commemorate the death and resurrection of Jesus.

Eusebius, writing in 336, shortly after the event, describes with gusto the discovery of the site:

> As one layer after another was laid bare, the place beneath the earth appeared. Then forthwith, contrary to all expectation, did the venerable and hallowed monument of our Saviour's resurrection become visible, and the most holy cave received what was an exact emblem of His coming to life.. No power of language seems worthy to describe the wonder.... The token of that most holy passion, long ago buried underground (had) remained unknown for so many cycles of years, until it should shine forth to His servants.[1]

Purple passages abound in Eusebius: it is difficult to distinguish facts from eloquence.So the site was unknown. How was it found? One version says Helena was 'divinely directed by dreams'.[2] Another says a nameless Jew 'derived his information from some documents come to him by paternal inheritance', and then, with disarming naïveté adds, 'but it seems more accordant with truth to suppose that God revealed the fact by means of signs and dreams'.[3]

This revealing quotation comes perhaps a hundred years after the event. A century later the story has gained some nice circumstantial details.

The Empress, *it is said*, had a divine vision. The Bishop, when he heard, went out to meet her accompanied by his suffragan bishops. *When all were at a loss* what to do, and each suggested a different thing, acting on *mere conjecture*, Bishop Macarius bade them all to be of a quiet mind and offer heartfelt prayers to God. When this was done the place was *miraculously revealed* to the Bishop, being that wherein the figure of the most unclean goddess stood.[4] (*Italics mine*)

The 'unclean goddess' was Venus. The version usually related nowadays explains that the Emperor Hadrian, in order to insult the Christians, had built a temple to Venus on the known site of the crucifixion, thus inadvertently preserving the memory of the very thing which he wished to obliterate. (This is not unlikely; Hadrian almost certainly did something similar at Bethlehem and unwittingly preserved Christ's birthplace. In a comparable move he erected another pagan shrine on the site of the Jewish temple.)

But in that case, there would have been no difficulty in *finding* the place. They simply had to demolish the shrine, as they did in Bethlehem. So why the ignorance, the mystery, the search, and the need for miraculous disclosures?

The embroidery continues as years pass. Helena, it was said, found not only the hill of Calvary and the tomb, but the three crosses (Christ's and the two thieves') buried nearby in a water cistern. You will be shown the cistern today, deep under the church, its walls entirely covered with little carved crosses where pilgrims have left their marks from far-off countries. But the story is an absurdity. The wood could not have been preserved. The crosses could not have been identified and kept in the first place: crosses were used and re-used for a succession of victims. Most serious of all, a complete cross was not something that was moved. The upward stem would simply be a standing tree (the New Testament repeatedly says it was: Acts 5:30; 10:39; 13:29; Gal. 3:13; 1 Pet. 2:24). The cross-piece alone was mobile. It was carried through the streets by the victim, with the accusation nailed to it. It was *this* that Jesus, after two beatings, was unable to carry.

So the story meanders on. What becomes clear is that Bishop Macarius very much wanted money for a new church, and Helena very much wanted to find the sites of biblical events. The contemplation of some of the characteristics of Roman and Byzantine church power-struggles is not an exercise calculated to increase confidence in the facts and the motives involved in erecting a lavish and luxurious shrine to the Saviour's suffering.

However, erect it they did – and in the process effectively ruined any chance of preserving evidence in support of the site's choice.

The hill thought to be Calvary was actually cut back to one thirty-foot cube of rock and then overlaid with marble. The nearby tomb-area was similarly treated; most of the rocky hillside cut away leaving one hollow cube which was then carved into lavish shapes and decorated. A huge domed basilica was then built over both areas. Later the tomb was completely destroyed by ravaging Persians, and had to be rebuilt.

The present erection pointed out as the tomb of Christ in no way fits the Gospel narrative, and is owned by one oriental group. There is a tiny alternative tomb tacked on the back by a rival hierarchy. Altogether five churches stake their claim to the shrine: Greek Orthodox, Roman Catholic, Syrian Jacobite, Armenian and Coptic. Interminable arguments rage over who owns what. For centuries two Muslim families have kept the keys, to keep warring factions apart and punch-ups to a minimum. The unfortunate Ethiopians have been expelled by their co-religionists, and live in mud huts on the roof.

Visually, the Holy Sepulchre offers nothing. There is no execution-hill, no garden, no road where passers mocked, no rolling-stone tomb, no ledge on which the body lay. It is well inside the city wall in a heavily built-up area. If the wall in Jesus' time was really much further in to the south (as advocates of the Holy Sepulchre have to assert), then the site might just have been barely outside, as both Bible account and Roman custom demand. That puts the wall along a hypothetical line that would make it virtually indefensible, with higher ground dominating it from the outside.

It is all just possible. A hundred years before Christ, the wall was much further in, that is certain. The area was at one time a burial ground outside the city. I once clambered behind a piece of broken wall (left unrepaired for decades by quarrelling ecclesiastics fearful of acceding 'rights' to rival sects) and found myself in an eerie region which archaeologists have since told me was an ancient quarry. Several *khokhim* (oven-like graves) penetrate the sides of the quarry. This was the commonest form of burial. But Jesus was quite specifically *not* buried in such a grave, rather in a wealthy man's sepulchre (an arcosolium, or vaulted tomb). Although I have not seen them, I am assured that evidence of such tombs has also been found in the area. The Gospel account infers one private burial-chamber standing alone in a private garden, not a well used public burial-ground in a quarry (see Luke 23:50-53).

Excavations (wherever possible) since 1960 have gradually added evidence that the area was indeed a mixture of gardens and burial grounds outside the city wall, and adjoining the Roman road. Dr. Dan Bahat has expressed to me his conclusion that (I quote) we may not be absolutely certain that this is the site of Jesus' burial, but we certainly have no other site that can lay a claim nearly as weighty, and we really have no reason to reject its authenticity. He once had a private audience with the Pope and told him the same!

In the long run, the Holy Sepulchre's most impressive argument is simply that it is there. It has been there a very long time. Most Christians throughout most of history have assumed it is the very place. A vast volume of devotion, worship, contemplation and passion has focused on this spot. I shall take the reader to a place that appeals to me more and which offers a visual impact impossible in this dusty crowded mausoleum. But that too falls well short of offering decisive and final evidence. Perhaps God wants it that way. For the *fact* of Christ's death and resurrection is totally central to Christianity, but the *place* is of no vital consequence. In that death and rising, God was acting decisively for the world's salvation and for mine. That is where faith takes its stand, love gathers its energy, and worship finds its motive.

I watch a woman thinly clad, her face lined with age and care. She kneels over the stone that supposedly marks the place where Jesus' body was brought down from the cross for anointing. She repeatedly kisses the stone with rapt gaze. Idolatry? No – why should it be that? Who but the Holy Spirit can give her such love for the Saviour? What but the reality of his suffering for her (wherever it happened) can give her relief and peace?

A black-robed priest intones a chant in the supposed place where the cross was laid to take its sacred burden. I know him. As a teenager in far-off Greece he became possessed of a desire above all else to live and pray at the place where Jesus died. His parents tried to dissuade him, and he threat-

ened to run away. Years of intensive training followed. Now
he lives out his days and years, caught up in a pageant of
cyclic praise and meditation which is foreign to my inclina-
tion and experience but in which I can recognise a man touching the eternal. Can anyone doubt that the love of Christ con-
strains him?

Gordon's Calvary

My first view of the rival Calvary site was as accidental as
my first sight of the Holy Sepulchre. Four of us were getting
to know Jerusalem for the first time, and without the assist-
ance of a professional guide we were making a singular mud-
dle of it. One of my friends grabbed my arm as we wandered
through the archways of the Damascus Gate and found ourselves outside the walls in Arab East Jerusalem. 'Look –
shape of a skull! It *must* be!' We dodged hooting buses in the
crowded bus terminus and stood below a forty foot cliff gazing upwards. Variegated limestone made odd shapes where
erosion had worn away the softer stone and left the harder.
Calvary. Golgotha. Roman and Hebrew for *skull*.

Could this be where Jesus died? If it was, where was the
garden? John tells us that 'Carrying his own cross, he went
out to the Place of the Skull. Here they crucified him.... At
the place where Jesus was crucified, there was a garden and
in the garden a new tomb... they laid Jesus there' (John 19:17,
41, 42).

We had all heard vaguely of the Garden Tomb beside
Gordon's Calvary. I recalled a hero-preacher from my teens,
a chaplain with the Mission to Mediterranean Garrisons, with
tales of serving soldiers who had encountered Jesus in that place.

Excited questions addressed to passers-by elicited indif-
ferent shrugs and curt denials. No one, it seemed, had heard

of the place. 'If it *is* the spot, they still treat it the same,' I commented. 'Is it nothing to you, all ye that pass by?'

Eventually, with help from a map, we took three right turns through crowded streets, and found a doorway in a high wall which brought us back to the hill at a higher level. Inside the doorway a garden of astonishing greenery beckoned us. The Garden Tomb. There was bustle everywhere. Paths zig-zagged amongst the flowers below the giant Jerusalem pines, amongst the palms and pomegranates. Groups of tourists filled every path. Somewhere in the near-distance voices were lifted in song – two songs – no, three, and in different languages. A blonde young man with Scandinavian accent offered to show us round. He quoted the Bible with simple conviction. He spoke of Jesus, as of a personal friend.

We found ourselves on a viewing platform above the bus-station, gazing across at Skull Hill again. Yes – two eye-sockets, a suggestion of a nose, even a few broken teeth. The guide explained.

This is undoubtedly an ancient Jewish execution site. Bet-ha-Sekilah (one of its names) means Place of Stoning. Execution was carried out, according to the Talmud, by casting the victim down from a cliff top and dropping a boulder from the height on to his chest. Appointed men called the witnesses performed this task. Hopefully, the first fall killed him, but afterwards the general public could join in with rocks and stones to complete the job. Of Stephen's martyrdom we read: 'They began to stone him. Meanwhile *the witnesses* laid their clothes at the feet of a young man named Saul' (Acts 7:58).

Eusebius, the church historian, describes the stoning of James the Just, leader of the Jerusalem Church and Jesus' brother:

Accordingly they went up and *cast the Just down*. They said to one
another, 'Let us stone James the Just', and they began to stone him.
Since he was not killed by the fall, he turned and knelt down saying, 'I beseech thee, Lord God Father, forgive them for they know
not what they do'.[5]

Our guide went on to reason that the most likely place for the
Romans to carry out their form of execution was in an al-
ready-used Jewish execution site. It seems likely. The crosses
would already stand there, needing only the grim cross-piece
carried to the site by the condemned victims. For Jewish
law required the bodies of stoned criminals to be hanged or
displayed on poles or trees afterwards, so that all might witness the completion of the sentence. Deuteronomy describes
this, and Paul writing to the Galatians links the custom and
its significance with the cross of Christ, in astonishing words
that go right to the heart of the gospel: 'Christ redeemed us
from the curse of the law by becoming a curse for us, for it is
written: "Cursed is everyone who is hanged on a tree" '
(Gal. 3:13; Deut. 21:23).

The guide was a sensitive young man, with a love for
Christ that shone on his face. (Incidentally, although I later
went to live and work at the Garden, I could never discover
who he was. There were no records of any of the staff being
as young as he was, and long-standing workers there denied
any knowledge of him. Do some angels have Scandinavian
accents, I wonder?) He offered no guarantees. This *may* be
the place. It fits the biblical references (they could hardly be
called descriptions) in several respects. It provides a remarkable visual aid. It throws light on some of the puzzling
details. Most of all, it turns our attention to Jesus. Why did
he die? Just over there (pointing) lies the Temple Mount. On
its slopes tens of thousands of sacrifices have been offered

that could no more than hopefully *symbolise* the taking away of sin. But Jesus offered one sacrifice for sin – once and for all – and the work was done. Reality. Pardon. New beginnings.

Rita and I held hands and quietly wept. It was one of those spiritual experiences that sometimes come unbidden, and form no necessary part of the life of faith but are welcome bonuses of grace. We offered ourselves again to the service of Christ, wherever that might take us. We offered our sons and their children to come. Not in our wildest dreams did we imagine that part of God's acceptance of our offer would be to send us back to live in this place and occupy an open-air pulpit beside an empty tomb from which we would share the gospel story with international thousands.

Cross and controversy

The Garden Tomb Association themselves make modest claims. Their little illustrated brochure, which sells in thousands, simply describes it as an Herodian tomb in an area regarded by many people as the garden of Joseph of Arimathea. The Association acts as trustees for land originally bought by Archbishop Benson of Canterbury in 1880. The story is a fascinating one.

In 1867 the Greek owner of this area, encouraged by certain clues, began to dig in search of a possible water cistern. It was there to be found, but he dug in the wrong place and discovered instead what he took to be an old cave. He put it into use as a garden shed, but the garden never came into being for the hoped-for water cistern remained hidden.

Along came a German archaeologist and philanthropist called Conrad Schick. What he saw excited him. 'This,' he said, 'is a tomb from the Herodian period.' Several explorers

were unimpressed at this time by the claims of the Holy
Sepulchre, and at least two other tombs north of the present
city wall were regarded as possibilities for the tomb of Jesus.

Interest lapsed – until General ('Chinese') Gordon came
on the scene. This moody, mystical Victorian hero adventurer and Christian soldier was only a year short of his ill-
fated military mission to Khartoum where violent death
awaited him. He stayed with friends whose house stood on
the northern city wall, beside the old Roman road, and opposite what is now the bus station. According to legend, he
noticed the hill's resemblance to a skull, and pronounced it
to be Calvary. That is a shorthand version. In actual fact he
came with his calculations already made and his conclusions already reached. His thinking was based on a complicated 'typology' much in vogue at that time, which saw detailed symbolic and prophetic significance in every detail of
the Old Testament ritual. To Gordon, Calvary had to be north
of the Temple Mount, and the skull must be part of a crucifixion figure as viewed from the sky above the city. His reasoning is something of an embarrassment nowadays. Nevertheless, the hill does look like a skull, several Protestant
scholars had already said so, and Gordon *did* point it out
with renewed vigour. People suddenly recalled that five minutes walk away was a Herodian tomb.

The General went off to his martyrdom and into the pages
of popular history. His letter home describing Skull Hill created a sensation. A full excavation of the neglected tomb
was launched, and results were startling. Most tombs are
natural caves, but this is carved out of rock – as the Bible
describes (Matt. 27:60). Rolling-stone tombs are rare, but
this one has a channel cut across the floor in front of the door
which may have been the runner for such a stone, although

that is not how similar tombs were designed. It has two chambers: one for burial and the other for mourners to watch and weep before the interment. Several Gospel incidents make it clear that a space such as this must have existed (e.g. Luke 24:2-3). Unusually, the burial chamber is on the right inside the door, instead of beyond the weeping-chamber – exactly how Mark describes it (Mark 16:5). John vividly relates how, on Easter morning, he hesitated to step inside, but peered in from the doorway and could see from that position the winding-cloths lying discarded (John 20:3-5). To look in this way would be impossible in any other known tomb in Jerusalem, but is exactly appropriate of the Garden Tomb. One of the most impressive moments for any visitor is to imitate John's movements and see how they correspond to the Gospel account.

There are several evidences of early Christian use of the tomb as some kind of shrine, but this was in the Byzantine period. The position in relation to Skull Hill is correct (if indeed Skull Hill is Calvary). And that elusive water-cistern turned up in a later excavation. It is massive – the size of a parish church – yet carved out of solid rock to store one quarter million gallons of rainwater, thus making a garden possible (John 19:41). Later still a splendidly preserved wine-press was found. Both date from the correct period.

Visually, the whole thing is perfect. Archaeologically, the case is not as overwhelming as it seems, and historically it is weak. Admittedly the English pioneer archaeologist Katherine Kenyon described it as a Herodian tomb, but more recent opinion declares it to be far too old; a very typical example of 'first temple period' centuries before Christ. Does it really matter? Not a bit.

The *historical* fact that Jesus was crucified in the cir-

cumstances related in the Bible is so overwhelmingly clear
that one could only question or deny it if one's mind were
already darkened by the wish that it had never happened.
The *theological* meaning depends on factors totally outside
historical and archaeological proof. Only the Spirit of God
can teach a man or woman to say, 'He loved me and gave
himself for me.' The *geographical* location has nothing to
do with either. To be able to point to a spot of earth and say
'He died here' is no step at all towards saying 'He died for
me'. *That* is the cry of faith.

As a visual aid to the essential Gospel story, the Garden
Tomb is as superb as the Holy Sepulchre is abysmal. But
that comment is quite subjective. Some people are as moved
by candles and incense, crumbling stones and chanting priests,
as I am by a rocky hill, a garden of greenery and a rock-
hewn tomb. What matters is that we take our place, with
penitence, faith and adoration, at the foot of a cross which
does not now stand on a square yard of Palestinian soil, but
towers over a suffering, sinning world with the offer of pardon and peace with God.

I have a colourful imagination when awake, and dream
technicolor dreams of mystifying complexity when I sleep.
But never, waking or sleeping, did I dream the first ten times
I visited Gordon's Calvary and the Garden Tomb that for
fifteen unforgettable months they would constitute my home
and my church. There we saw what successive chaplains,
directors, chairmen and guides have seen since it was opened
to the public in 1895.

Men and women from a bewildering variety of nations
came and looked and listened – and found faith restored or
newly created, in the Garden.

For the tomb is empty. Wherever the authentic grave is, it

housed its precious guest for only parts of three days. Then
Jesus rose and went. He did not leave it totally empty. The
grave-clothes, still wrapped and interleaved with spices,
lay abandoned. No grave-robbers had unwrapped them. The
body came *through* them, as it came through the stone and
through closed doors. (The rolling stone was not moved to
let him out – how could it keep him in? It was moved to
allow the disciples in, to discover that Christ had risen!)
And a small significant detail: the headcloth lay folded in a
place of its own (John 20:3-7). Jesus was a carpenter; when
a craftsman in his time had finished a task for his customer,
he washed his hands on a napkin, folded it and left it beside
the finished task. The symbolic message was 'job done'.

And so it was – gloriously and completely. 'Jesus said,
"It is finished". With that he bowed his head and gave up his
spirit' (John 19:30).

> Lifted up was He to die,
> 'It is finished' was His cry,
> Now in Heaven exalted high,
> Hallelujah, what a Saviour.[6]

References

1. Eusebius, *Life of Constantine*, Chapter 3:28-30.
2. Socrates, *Historia Ecclesiastica*, Chapter 1:17.
3. Sozomen, *Historia Ecclesiastica*, Chapter 2:1.
4. Alexander Monachus, *The Invention of the Holy Cross*.
5. Eusebius, *Ecclesiastical History* 2:23. Josephus also briefly records
the event, and dates it as AD 61. *Antiquities of the Jews* 20:9-10.
6. Philip Bliss, the hymn, 'Man of Sorrows'.

12

Witness of the Empty Tomb

One of the guides grabbed my arm. 'I'm sure that's George Kennedy!' 'Pardon?' 'George Kennedy! You know – one of the Magnificent Seven. Remember those marvellous cowboy films that always had Yul Brynner in them. Kennedy's the one that shot the noose off his friend's neck just as they were hanging him!'

He was right, too, my friend with the encyclopaedic knowledge of Hollywood westerns. I recognised the man myself now, although I didn't recall the incident of the noose. Very big, a splendidly brutal face, and legs that looked positively odd without a horse between them. He and his slim blonde wife asked me to show them around, and soon we were inspecting the wine-press, looking out over Skull Hill, stooping to enter the tomb. As we came out again, blinking in the sunshine, I said, 'Of course we don't insist that this is the very place. And it really doesn't matter. Nothing depends on finding *where* Christ died – everything depends on discovering *why* he did it.'

I glanced at them to see their reaction, and gently pushed a little more. 'Even the arguments for the resurrection, although very impressive, can never be wholly conclusive. There has to be faith. In the long run it's like this: an old hymn poses the question, "You ask me how I know he lives..."' The film star's wife interrupted with a big grin and finished the quotation for me 'He lives within my heart!' She squeezed her husband's arm: 'And he does, too – he lives in both of us.' I laughed with delight, and we all hugged each other. Just another incident in the seemingly endless succession of passing encounters at the Garden Tomb.

The apostle Paul once said on a dramatic occasion, 'I stand here and testify to small and great alike... that the Christ would suffer and (be) first to rise from the dead' (Acts 26:22-23). Our circumstances were very different, but the purpose was the same. Bishop Arthur Goodwin-Hudson used to describe the Garden Tomb as 'the world's greatest Gospel visual-aid'.

There, life-size, was an execution site outside Jerusalem's city wall, a skull-shaped hill, a rich man's garden, a rolling stone tomb. People came in their hundreds; individuals and families, pilgrimages and tour-groups, twenty at a time, two hundred at a time, often over a thousand in one working day. All heard the gospel story in its simplicity.

American sailors on shore-leave, European schoolchildren on a Mediterranean cruise, church groups led by pastors and priests, United Nations peace-keeping troops from Sinai and Golan, Japanese businessmen, Africans in gorgeous flamboyant robes, West Indians who have rushed back to the hotel to dress in white before coming to the garden – in they poured, round they walked, whispering, chattering, singing, staring... sometimes crying.

At one level we were simply a tourist-trap, a point on most people's itinerary because we qualified for that curious accolade, an Israeli government 'registered holy site' (the only Protestant one, at that!). At another level, without any disguise, we operated as a gentle evangelistic agency that contented itself with simply stating the biblical and historical facts, illustrating them visually, and answering people's questions. Peter's well-known words (one of my mottoes since teenage years) really summed it up: 'Always be prepared to give an answer to everyone who asks you to give the reason for the hope that you have ... with gentleness and respect' (1 Pet. 3:15-16).

One day, for example, our son Paul was taking round an American church group. The area around the tomb was crowded as they approached, so he stood by the wine-press and said, half-jokingly, 'We shall have to wait here for a few minutes: if it was a bit longer I might preach you a sermon!' The group-leader piped up, 'Why not?' Paul spoke for five minutes on the meaning of the words 'Christ died for our sins', and finished with 'In the long run, what matters is not the site of the empty tomb, but a sight of the One who left it empty'. Two girl hikers, drifting around the youth hostels, had listened from the edge of the crowd. Pushing forward, they asked how they might commit their lives to Christ.

Living in very different style was the visiting group of politicians and businessmen from an American state, both Jewish and Gentile. The state governor was one of them, and for the sake of 'security' we arranged a private viewing. Some of them wished to stay for the open-air service held weekly. One of the governor's security agents seemed new to the job: he spent much of the sermon buttoning and unbuttoning his jacket, and easing his gun in and out of its shoulder-holster. Suddenly there was a very loud bang. It often happens: Israeli fighter planes patrolling the Jordanian border, sweep up over the Judaean wilderness and break the sound barrier. People unaccustomed to it do have a tendency to dive for cover. Several in the congregation did so now, and the nervous agent did a splendid Starsky and Hutch imitation, leaping in front of the governor, knees in crouch position, arms out stiff, automatic pistol held two-handed.

It did tend to interrupt the flow of the sermon, which was entitled 'Jesus – the Man we cannot ignore'. I paused and explained. 'Don't be distressed. If you hear a loud bang, always listen for the sound of an aeroplane afterwards. If you can hear it, there's nothing to worry about. If you can't hear anything, it's too late!'

There was a lot of hearty laughter, the agent sheepishly put his gun away, and the sermon continued. Afterwards one of the party, proprietor and editor of a major American newspaper, told me, 'This morning I have rediscovered my childhood faith. Thank you. If you ever come to the States, I'd like you to visit with me.'

I wasn't too sure what that peculiarly American phrase 'visit with me' meant, but when I took him up on it a year later I found myself as his guest, invited to speak to the civic and business heads of a famous city. One of them testified to the others that his life had been completely 'changed' by that visit to the garden. A local Baptist pastor who took me to the meal whispered, white-faced with excitement, 'Do you realise what you've got here? The financial, political and social power of this city.' It led to more – a great deal more at a higher level still, but name-dropping is not my concern. 'I testify to small and great alike...'

The Anglican writer and preacher D R Davies used to describe the church sermon as 'twenty minutes to raise the dead'. We normally had about five minutes more than that to take a group around the site, explain the natural features, the archaeological arguments, the historical facts – and to show how God did in fact raise the dead. Sometimes it was a good deal less. Everyone has heard of those lightning tours so beloved by Americans. One party leader wrote to me recently with the outline of a proposed Christian Heritage

Holiday in Britain. It included for Day 2 (I quote): 'Tour of Ireland, ferry to Scotland, preliminary tour of Scotland...'

Some of the Mediterranean tours are rather like this. They include a ship's arrival at Haifa, and a day's tour of Israel. Two hours are given to Jerusalem. The Garden Tomb gets ten minutes, and as we had the city's cleanest 'washrooms' (as the Americans call toilets) there was usually a rush for them.

I never actually heard an Israeli version of the fabled phrase, 'It's Tuesday so this must be Paris', but I do recall one lady who trudged up the path with her lightning-tour group, and asked me dazedly, 'What country is this?'

We usually managed to negotiate fifteen minutes *plus* the washroom visit. Was it worth it? Some of our governing committee doubted it. But after all, words of Scripture form the living Word of God, the divine seed that produces life in the responsive heart. Even very small seed can produce a very big plant, as Jesus illustrated from the parable of the mustard seed (Matt. 13:31-32).

We grew that tree at the garden, and I would often pass the tiny seeds on to visitors and silently pray that the few words I said would have the same effect. When it did, we sometimes heard: more often we knew nothing of the harvest.

During the heat of the summer, when few tourists come, I flew home to Britain and preached at the Keswick Bible Convention. One lady there told me a story.

'Four months ago I was on one of those whistle-stop Mediterranean tours. I found, to my embarrassment that most of the passengers were high-spending and hard-drinking brewers and their wives. We had one day in Israel, and I asked the guide to show us the Garden Tomb. He refused, but several couples became curious, and insisted. Five days later, in an Athens hotel, some of us were sitting in the hotel lounge discussing the holiday and what had impressed us most. One wealthy woman said, "Well, that missionary place, the Garden Tomb, interested me more than anything else. I won't forget it for a long time." A brewer's wife quietly chipped in: "I shan't *ever* forget it. It has changed my life. I became a Christian while we were there." '

At the same Convention, a group of Christians from Cornwall told me, 'A wealthy woman from our little village came back from a Holy Land holiday last winter. She amazed everyone by telling them that she had become a convinced Christian through visiting the Tomb. She has plunged into all kinds of witnessing, and has already made a real impact on the district.'

Worship the King
Of course many were already convinced and committed before they came. I estimate that half of the thousand-a-day visitors are evangelical or charismatic Christians who make the visit to the Garden Tomb the high point of their tour. Half a dozen large and small worship areas are landscaped into the one-acre garden, usually grouped around a stone communion table. All six will often be in use at one time, and the murmur of prayers, the reading of Scripture, the singing of hymns in several different languages, mingle in the air with a quiet harmony that seems to signal that Pentecost has stood the Tower of Babel on its head and given all believers one common tongue of prayer and praise. Words like *Hallelujah* and *Jesus* sound very much the same in French, Chinese, Polish and Swahili!

A huge black man with gleaming teeth, a gold crown on his head, a purple robe and an orange cummerbund, introduces himself as the Archbishop of the Marching Church of Zimbabwe with Signs Following. The worship of his group is a fascinating mixture of Anglican liturgy and charismatic improvisation; at one point they dance in an opening and closing circle, the men stamping their feet and the women ululating: it is like a scene from Rider Haggard. In contrast, stolid German believers sing a sombre hymn with lovely humming harmony that I suspect comes straight from Martin Luther.

A large party of Japanese from some new sect ask if they might hold a service in front of the tomb. I used my discretion, and suggested they come at lunchtime when the Garden is closed to visitors; someone had warned me they are rather noisy. That proved to be something of an understatement. I have never heard a cacophony quite like it: hooting, babbling, shouting. It actually brought Arabs running up the lane and climbing the wall on each other's shoulders, to see what was going on. I had given them thirty minutes, but wondered however I was going stop them. No need to worry.

Exactly on the dot, their leader glanced at his watch, shouted a word of command and instantly, in full flight, surely halfway through a sentence, the noise stopped. They smiled and marched out in silence. Their leader handed me a box of chocolate biscuits from Japan with much bowing. Bemused, I slipped into a returning-the-bow routine, to which he replied with a bow and I responded with another, and he repaid the compliment again, and.... in true Peter Sellers fashion I realised that the only way to bring it to an end was for me to stop. My son fell about laughing in the background and a new joke was added to the impressive family record: 'Did you hear the one about the Japanese chocolate biscuits?'

Humour was a great releaser of tension. The Garden Tomb

caters for ever-increasing numbers of people, a small percentage of whom show all the unreasonableness, bad manners and outrageous demands that any shop assistant experiences. The key is to keep cool at the time but turn each bad experience into a joke afterwards. Once the gate was closed, we were bursting to relate incidents, and tease each other for the way we handled or mishandled them.

There was the man with the flowing beard and big stick who sometimes stood just outside and silently gave out religious tracts. Now and again he became convinced that he was Elijah. Storming inside, he would shake his cudgel at the staff and call us 'paper Christians'. There was the American televangelist who arrived with two hundred followers, four carrying a coffin-like box full of prayers written on slips of paper. 'A thousand who could not come here paid ten dollars each to have their prayers read at Calvary,' he said. He got short shrift.

The Garden Tomb Association has as one of its stated aims protection of the area from 'commercialism and superstition'. We coldly pointed out that Calvary (if indeed Skull Hill is that) stands outside our garden, in the Arab bus station. We discovered afterwards that the evangelist had stood on the city wall 200 yards from the cliff, and with some artful camera angles had contrived to give the impression that he was 'at Calvary'. It is, after all, the image that counts. And the dollars, of course.

A group of Caribbean Christians poured in – lovely, simple, happy people. All of them were very heavily built. Our guide finished his peroration with his favourite words: 'Let me tell you the most wonderful thing about the tomb of Jesus wherever it is – *it is empty*!'

The most buxom lady in the crowd let out a whoop of

'Hallelujah!', turned an astonishing cartwheel, then attempted
a second one, and landed upside down in a flowering shrub,
legs waving in the air. Hauled out by her friends, she smiled
placidly as if nothing had happened, and gave her attention
to the last few words from the startled guide.

One of us explained to a quiet group of Canadians that
this may be the garden of Joseph of Arimathea. A lady interrupted to ask, 'Wasn't that the one with the coat of many
colours?' 'No dear,' intervened her husband, 'he means the
man that started the Mormons.'

My son, in clowning mood, with a particularly friendly
group, decided to tease them. He said solemnly, 'One very
impressive proof we have found is a tree with a heart carved
on it, and the words, "Joseph loves Mrs Arimathea".' A few
chuckled, but Paul had the feeling that the joke didn't click.
After their walk, one minister's wife came to him perfectly
seriously and asked to be shown the tree – she'd love to
have a photograph!

Two of the staff overheard a particularly brilliant piece
of tact from me (they assure me with gasps of mock-admira-
tion). Someone had just asked me if General Gordon still
lives here (he died just over a hundred years ago). I gravely
explained that, 'The Gordon family are not directly respon-
sible for the Garden nowadays.' That won the current award
for Answer of the Week.

Someone else was very insistent that last time he came,
ten years ago, he heard General Gordon preach here. At first
he got quite vexed at my suggestion that this wasn't possible, but we avoided further argument when I wondered aloud
whether it might have been Colonel Dobbie, and he acknowl-
edged that it could have been. It was a soldier anyway.

The inevitable know-all who has been before kept assuring his friends that the whole thing was a con-trick; it appeared that we had altered the layout since he last came. In fact we have had to widen and re-route one of the paths because of increasing numbers of visitors. He seemed to think that someone assured him last time that the body of Jesus was carried along this very track. Now he suddenly asserted that we had 'moved the stone'. I pricked up my ears, for Morrison's splendid book *Who Moved the Stone?* is a favourite of mine. 'You mean the stone from the door of the tomb? No, we've never had that there – it wasn't found in 1867, when the tomb was rediscovered.'

'Nonsense,' shouted the pest. 'It was here ten years ago, I tell you. You've altered everything.'

'Tell you what,' I suggested, 'when you get home, look up your holiday snaps. If you can find one with the stone on it, send me it in the post, and I'll pay you fifty dollars for it.' He seemed satisfied, and of course, I never heard from him again.

Curiously, at least twenty people have assured me at different times that they saw the rolling-stone last time they were here. Possibly they have confused memories of the Herod family tomb on the western slope of the city, a fine example of this kind of tomb, and one of the very few available for inspection. Most people were buried in a *kokh*. The Hebrew word means 'oven' and refers to an oven-like aperture cut out of the rock, just large enough for a body to be slid horizontally into it. The little opening was then blocked with stone and clay. But the Gospel records speak clearly of a large vaulted tomb for Jesus' burial (John 19:41) having room for several people (and angels!) to stand inside, and closed with a 'great stone' (Matt. 27:60). This is exactly in accord with what we know of a rich man's burial, and of course, Joseph of Arimathea, a member of the ruling Sanhedrin, was a wealthy man.

The stone could be held in place by a number of different devices; at Herod's Tomb an arch holds it in place; at the Garden Tomb a low sloping wall about nine inches high runs across the doorway, eighteen inches in front of it and slightly bevelled around the outside edge to fit this shape. Dame Katherine Kenyon, the British pioneer archaeologist who confirmed the approximate dating and style of the Garden Tomb, calculated that the stone itself was unnaturally large. It probably stood seven feet high, eighteen inches thick, and weighed about seven tons.

These impressive figures are important. One of the earliest 'explanations' for the empty tomb on the first Easter day was the charge that the disciples moved the stone, stole the body, and then pretended that Jesus had risen. Matthew mentions where the story came from; the Sanhedrin bribed the guards to 'admit' that they fell asleep on duty and the disciples took that opportunity. We have independent evidence of this story in the North African world of the early second century, where Tertullian, the converted lawyer, came across it.

I once took a large crowd of Ghanaian UN soldiers to the tomb entrance, and gave them a short lecture on evidence for the resurrection. 'Do you know what the penalty was for a Roman soldier sleeping on duty?' I asked.

There was a buzz of speculation, and then I told them. Execution.

'Can you imagine them going to sleep with *that* hanging over them? The Bible uses a technical phrase – there was a *squad* of them, as we would say. Fourteen. So all fourteen have to nod off. All at once, mind you – so that not one is left

awake to shake the others awake again for fear of being executed.'

The tough troops saw the point clearly enough, and I
warmed to my argument.

'Take your imagination a bit further. They all have to not
only nod off, but fall so deeply asleep that a gang of Galileans
can come along with ropes and pulleys, block and tackle, *and
move seven tons of stone without waking a single one up*!'

They were laughing and nodding now.

'Imagine those sentries giving their evidence later. The
judge asks them what happened. They say that those rotten
Nazarenes came along and pulled a fast one. How do you
know? they would be asked. What's your evidence? And out
comes the classic answer: Your honour, we know because
we were eye-witnesses. We were there when it happened –
er – fast asleep!'

The Africans burst out laughing, slapping each other's
backs and clapping.

'You see, all that story from the guards actually *proves* is
that the tomb really was empty. Otherwise why give a story
to account for its emptiness?'

I held out my hands appealingly.

'What have we got then? An empty tomb and a daft explanation that explains nothing. How does the *Bible* explain it?
St. Paul sums it up in one sentence, at the end of Romans
chapter four. He says, "He was delivered over to death for
our sins, and was raised to life for our justification" (Rom.
4:25). I like to put it simply like this: at the cross, the Son of
God paid the price for our sins. At the empty tomb the Father
wrote the receipt underneath – *Received With Thanks*. Believe that. Pin all your hope to it. Ask God to bring the power
of it into your life.'

A young officer raised his hand. 'May I say something, sir?' He stepped out of the crowd and addressed the others. 'Men – what this man says is true. I believe it. I'm not ashamed of it. I want you all to believe it.'

They crowded round me to look at Bible verses, to get my autograph, to ask me to pray for them, to take copies of Scripture portions.

God was at work in the Garden, touching men's lives.

13

Build My Church

The south-western area of Jerusalem's Old City hides within its streets a fascinating secret. Here, if one knows where to look and how to interpret, is part of the answer to the question, 'What happened after the Tomb was found to be empty?'

Christian tourists usually find themselves whisked in and out in about twenty minutes. If on foot, they have probably walked through the restored Roman shopping street in the Jewish Quarter, and then passed through the wall at the Zion Gate. Their guide will have pointed out the shell-scars and bullet marks that bear silent witness to some of the bitterest fighting in 1948, when Israel was declared a Jewish State. If they arrived by bus, they will have come up the 'Pope's Road', built for the pontiff's visit when he came to view the puzzle which we now discuss.

The whole hill-side is covered in lovely arboreal gardens amongst which nestle Christian churches, monasteries and convents. There is no time to admire, as our guide hurries us on. We follow a high-walled lane that ends abruptly at a building which, even to the eye of the amateur, bears signs of having been built in a dozen different styles during many different centuries. A stern Orthodox Jew squatting in the doorway tells us to cover our heads if we are men, and our arms if we are women. We are about to visit the Tomb of David.

We crowd inside a small room and view through a protective railing a huge sarcophagus covered in purple velvet decorated

183

184 THETHE SAVIOUR

with Hebrew letters and symbols in gold and silver thread.
It seems to be standing in a curved niche of ancient stone that
is blackened as if by the smoke of ten thousand candles or
lamps. Individual Jewish worshippers sway and mutter as
they pray, whilst nervous tourists stare and whisper. On my
second visit, determined to observe more, I thought the rear
curving wall looked oddly like that of a church apse. It was
an idea with which I have subsequently become rather
pleased, for it holds one of the keys to this strange spot.

The guide whisks us out again within minutes. Blinking in
the sunshine, we hurry through a sun-baked courtyard full of
brilliant flowers in huge pots, past some elegant Spanish-
Morrocan arches. We dive through a gateway and plunge
indoors up a steep stone staircase that twists so often that
we lose any sense of direction when we emerge into a cool
corridor at the top. The door ahead brings us into a great
vaulted building of stone pillars supporting shallow domes
of ceiling, for all the world like one of those vaults discovered below some English Norman cathedral.

With a flourish our guide announces, 'This is the Upper
Room', adding some remark like, 'where Jesus held the Passo-
ver/ his Last Supper/ the first Mass' or 'where the Christian
Church was born'.

Several groups will be there at the same time. Catholics celebrate Mass in one corner. Protestants in another listen to a
reading from the Gospels. Pentecostalists speak in tongues with
even more than normal enthusiasm, since this is where that phenomenon first occurred.

We are bewildered. The arched hall cannot possibly be old
enough. Indeed, our guide mentions that it was built by Crusaders. Surely the city Jesus knew was destroyed in AD 70? Trying
to reconstruct our hurried journey of the last few moments, or

peering out of a window, we realise that we are standing directly above David's Tomb! How in the world can it be the Upper Room upstairs and the royal tomb downstairs? We shall try to remember to ask more when we reach our hotel. But no time now. The guide's schedule is slipping. We hurry back to the coach.

Winston Churchill once famously described Russia as a riddle wrapped in a mystery inside an enigma. The south-west hill, called Mount Zion since Crusader times, deserves that description. Disentangling the truth involves a detective exercise of some complexity. There are several clues including the Essenes who didn't live in the desert, the man who did a woman's job, the Christians who bravely ran away, the Roman soldiers who built a new camp, the burial site that kept moving, the synagogue that couldn't be there, the church that shifted sideways, and the scientist who was shot by terrorists. At the heart of the conundrum stands the place where the Christian Church was born.

'Church of the Apostles found on Mount Zion' shouted the title of a magazine article. Bargil Pixner is a devout and scholarly Benedictine monk who lives at the Dormition monastery on this very hill (in my opinion one of the most beautifully decorated Christian buildings in Israel). His article appeared in a magazine often given to zippy headlines like 'How Bad Was Ahab?', 'Something Fishy About Herod's Pool', 'Who Controls The Scrolls?', and 'Soup's On In A Talmudic Kitchen'. The magazine is American (need I add?). Despite the light-hearted headlines it is a reputable and scholarly publication supported by internationally famous archaeologists providing a popular shop-window for the more technical reports from the Bible-lands digs. What support does it give to the idea that a chamber on this highest point of

Jerusalem has links with Christ and his apostles?[1]

Readers of the New Testament will recall with ease the events that followed the resurrection appearances of Jesus. After his ascension from the Mount of Olives, his closest disciples returned joyfully to Jerusalem, there to worship and await the promised gift of the Holy Spirit (Luke 24:50-53; Acts 1:12-14). They met regularly in the 'Upper Room', where Jesus had delivered his final teaching before his death, celebrated his last Passover with them, and instituted the Lord's Supper or Communion (Luke 22:7-23; John 13-16). Here, it is usually assumed, he appeared to them alive after his death (John 20:19-31), and here they certainly gathered to plan and pray whilst they awaited 'the promise of the Father' (Acts 1:12-26).

Clearly it was a regular meeting place for the closest circle of disciples. Tradition and scholarship suggest that it may have been the home of Mary, John Mark's mother, who was a woman of some financial standing, living in the prestigious 'new city' west of the temple area.

Luke goes on to describe how, 'when the day of Pentecost came, they were all together in one place. Suddenly a sound like the blowing of a violent wind from heaven filled the whole house where they were sitting.... All of them were filled with the Holy Spirit' (Acts 2:1-4). As a result, a crowd gathered, Peter preached, and no less than 3,000 people repented and were baptised. We are then given a picture of the daily life of the growing infant church, with its shared faith, fellowship, sacrament and prayers (verses 37-45). They met in numbers great and small; the larger crowds in the temple courts and smaller groups in various houses (verses 46-48).

The early gatherings were made up of *Jewish* Christians, many of them very Jewish indeed. 'A large number of priests became obedient to the faith'; 'You see how many thousands of Jews have believed, and all of them are zealous for the law' (Acts 6:7; 21:20). James, a brother (or cousin) of Jesus became principal leader, and was renowned both inside and outside of the New Testament for his distinctively Hebrew piety.[2] It was only gradually and with some reluctance that the apostles came to understand that salvation through Jesus was available to Samaritans, to Gentile admirers of the Jewish faith (God-fearers), and even to complete pagans who were willing to turn, not to the Jewish religious practice, but to the grace of God (Acts 8, 10 and 15).

But why should we imagine that we can locate the very place where all of this began and for some years continued? And what has it to do with David's Tomb? We jump forward to the twentieth century. In the bitter fighting of 1948, the Israelis were forced out of the Jewish Quarter within the walls, but in turn forced the Arabs off the continuation of south-west hill outside the walls. The area became a dangerous and exposed frontier between Israel and Jordan. Before re-populating it, the Israelis asked an archaeologist, Jacob Pinkerfield, to excavate and examine the building for centuries described by Jews and Arabs as David's Tomb, and by Christians as the Upper Room. This had been damaged by a mortar shell during the fighting.

Tragically, the scholar was murdered in a terrorist attack on the Archaeological Convention of 1956, before his detailed findings could be published.

Pinkerfield found a succession of ever lower floor layers below the current floor. The most 'recent' was Crusader from the eleventh century, the next was early Byzantine or late Roman from the fifth or sixth century, and the oldest was early Roman from the second or third century. At the earliest

level, fallen plaster was pieced together and found to include
the words 'saviour', 'mercy' and 'Jesus'.

At this point early Christian authors come to our aid.
Writing in 315, Epiphanius, the Palestinian bishop of Salamis,
described how the emperor Hadrian visited the ruined city
in 130, after the failed rebellion led by Bar Kokba. Hadrian,
of course, was already planning his total rebuilding of the
city as a Roman metropolis called Aelia Capitolina. He found
that the only surviving buildings were 'a few houses, and the
little church of God on the spot where the disciples went to
the upper room on their return from the Mount of Olives
after the Ascension of the Redeemer. It was built on Zion,
which escaped the destruction'.[3]

A few years later, in 393, someone simply known as the
Bordeaux Pilgrim, described a single surviving 'synagogue'
inside Zion 'where David had his palace'.[4] This could not
possibly have been a functioning Jewish place of worship,
since all Jews had been banished after the failed rebellion.
The Tenth Legion actually occupied a semi-permanent camp-
fort on this very hill for years after. However, Jewish
Christians might well have been permitted to return for in
both the First Rebellion of 67-70 and the Second Rebellion
of 132-135 the Hebrew followers of Jesus (known at that
time as Nazarenes) refused to join the armed revolts. In the
first, they all left the city together, and crossed the Jordan for
refuge in the city of Pella, 'having been warned by an oracle'
(presumably Jesus' instruction, now found in Matthew 24:16,
to flee to the mountains).[5] During the second, they were
persecuted by the Jewish rebel leader, both for their pacifist
opposition to the war and for their refusal to acknowledge
him as Messiah.

Knowing all of this, the Romans seem to have regarded

Nazarenes as Christians rather than Jews politically, but Jews rather than Christians religiously, thus giving them the benefit of the doubt on two different scores! The word *synagogue* at that time was applied to early Christian gathering places, whether Jewish or Gentile; the word simply means prayer-place. It was only as the Gentile Christian majority drifted away from the Jewish minority that they began to use the alternative word *ecclesia* (church) to describe the building as well as the movement. There is therefore no puzzle about the fact that several early writers, not just those quoted, used 'synagogue', 'church' and 'house of God' to describe the same building on the western hill. It was a meeting place of Jewish followers of Jesus, believed to be associated with the very first Christian events.

Jump forward once more to the present century. Between 1948 and 1967 the Jews endured another Hadrianic-type expulsion, this time by the Jordanians. Because they lost their holiest site, the 'Wailing Wall', the building explored by Pinkerfield took on new significance. It was already reputed to mark David's tomb. True, that did not accord too well with their own Scriptures, which tell of his burial, and that of several royal successors, 'inside the city of David'.[6] But Jews, like Christians, understand that commemoration is more important than strict location; the site simply provides a locale for the recalling of the divine event. So what better place to become a centre of prayer than the tomb, or at least the monument, of that king who was described as a man after God's own heart?

The case of the mobile tomb
The actual original tomb had a patchy history. Its location was still known in Herod's time. Always on the lookout for

profit, he ordered its secret excavation in the hope of finding treasure. The diggers were frightened and two died mysterious deaths. The king changed his mind, abandoned the intrusion, and ordered an elaborate memorial to be erected instead. This, we must assume was the tomb referred to in Peter's Pentecost sermon: 'The patriarch David died and was buried, and his tomb is with us to this day' (Acts 2:29). The actual monument did not survive the Roman siege in AD 135, and its destruction was described by a Roman historian writing fifty years later.[7]

Burial inside the city was unusual, even irregular. Ritual cleansing and hygienic considerations normally precluded it. Rabbi Akiva, who supported the Bar Kokbah rebellion and proclaimed its leader as Messiah, was the last writer to claim certain knowledge of the tomb. He explained how physical purity in the case of the royal tombs was ensured by the presence of a channel running out of them and into the Kidron Valley. That fixed the location on the eastern side of the eastern hill, which as we have seen is precisely the site surprisingly pinpointed as David's citadel by modern archaeology.

In 1913 a French archaeologist Raymond Weill dug along the lower slope of the Ophel (Eastern) hill and found tombs of a superior design, with horizontal passages and chambers in the very area referred to by Akiva. The world of scholarship was not ready to adjust its thinking about the site of David's citadel at that time, and the tombs were allowed to be covered again and subsequently built over by Palestinians.

Modern Jews know perfectly well that David's tomb was 'moved' several times. After the Second Rebellion the expelled survivors relocated it for ritual reasons in

Bethlehem, David's birthplace. Christians happily accepted the idea, as Luke's Christmas account calls Bethlehem the city of David (Luke 2:11). Indeed they declared Jesse's resting place and Solomon's tomb to be there too, and organised pilgrimages to a cave near the reputed birthplace of Jesus. In due course Muslims accepted the idea too.

Perhaps because of that, Christians then felt another change of venue might be a good thing, and in the tenth century the south-western hill of Jerusalem became the favoured spot. This was now called Mount Zion, the name originally given to the eastern hill and then to the whole city. But this area already contained that site of the Upper Room, once called a 'little house of God'. Why not combine the two?

It was no longer 'little'. Christians had built an octagonal church alongside it in 382, and the whole complex became 'the Church of the Apostles'. Moreover, the split between Jewish and Gentile Christians in the city had sadly widened, especially after some very anti-semitic statements made at the Council of Nicaea. New purpose-built places of worship for the non-Jewish majority sprang up all over the city once the Roman empire became officially christianised.

In a famous sermon at the recently opened Church of the Holy Sepulchre, Cyril, soon to be Bishop of Jerusalem, dropped an intriguing comment. Speaking of the gift of the Holy Spirit, he remarked that his sermon would have been more appropriately given at 'the Upper Church of the Apostles', since *that* is where the Spirit was first given. The tradition was still intact.[8]

The building was greatly extended only thirty years later as a basilica-church of the kind favoured by Byzantine Christians. These were deliberate imitations of Roman public buildings. The message of the design (a large gathering-place for all, not a small temple for priests only) underlined the fact that Christians gathered to hear the Word of God and to celebrate Communion, not to stand outside whilst priests (pagan or Jewish) performed ceremonies. This building, called The Church of Holy Zion (Hagia Sion) had the original Church of the Apostles as a surviving annex incorporated in one corner. Presumably Jacob Pinkerfield's second-oldest floor reflects this development.

The third was laid when the Crusaders arrived. In 1110, they started again on the same site, and built the Church of St. Mary, slightly smaller than 'Holy Zion', but this time incorporating the Church of the Apostles into the main interior. It seemed sensible to provide a rather more distinguished 'upper room' on what no-one doubted was the authentic site of the New Testament events, and to lend it verisimilitude it was built one storey high. Directly below was a surviving apse or niche of the Holy Zion Church. The building was destined to stand for only 109 years of conflict between crusade and crescent. But here is Pinkerfield's most recent floor.

The enthusiastic Crusaders had another idea too. Why not commemorate King David here as well? Had not Peter, in his Pentecost sermon, inferred that David's tomb was nearby? A large Gothic cenotaph with an empty stone coffin was accordingly built to mark David's memory. A sensible place for it seemed to be in front of the curved apse of the older church; the very place that looked so suspiciously church-like to me (as to many others) when I first eyed it with some bewilderment.[9]

Then came another twist to the ironic tale. When the Crusaders were expelled again by the Muslims, Jews were welcomed back to the city, and had the opportunity to bring

David back with them, so to speak. With slowly increasing enthusiasm they claimed the Gothic sarcophagus left by the Crusaders. Muslims also assented to the notion. When the Caliph Omar ibn el-Khattab entered the city in triumph, his first request was to be shown the 'mihrah of David', that is the niche in the prayer-room of David.

Then came 1948. Once more the weary cycle of war expelled the Jews from the centre of the city and cut them off from their Prayer Wall. But not from Zion Hill, where stood David's tomb! Ever since then, its use and value has increased, even though the Wall is once more the central place of worship. Hence the man outside who presses little cardboard hats upon any visitor sufficiently insensitive to come with uncovered head. Hence, too, the guides' shorthand which gruffly announces downstairs 'David's Tomb' and upstairs 'the Upper Room', with little explanation.

The gate that was lost
Rita and I were enjoying a (Christian) Sabbath Dinner. Our hosts were the students and staff of the American School of Biblical Studies. This evangelical centre stands on the very tip of the South West Hill (Zion), next to the beautiful Dormitian Abbey and close to the Upper Room. The principal at that time, on loan from America's Wheaton Bible College, often supported my preaching-services at the Garden Tomb. After dinner and prayers I asked, 'Is it true that the so-called Essene Gate is in your grounds? Any chance of a look at it?'

He laughed. 'Sure! But what have you been reading? I don't often get asked that!'

We strolled through the hill-top garden, with its wonderful moonlit views over the southern valley and towards Bethlehem. We came to a depression in the ground, in which could just be seen either the lintel or the threshold of an ancient stone doorway. Jim Fleming had first alerted me to its significance by showing me a photograph whilst discussing the Qumran Essenes and the discovery of their Dead Sea Scrolls. Contrary to popular opinion, these devout people did not only live in desert communities; they had cells or settlements in most population centres. Josephus mentions a 'Gate of the Essenes' in Jerusalem 'in the south west corner of the city wall on the southwest hill'.[10]

These enthusiasts were welcomed to the city by Herod the Great, not for any religious reason but because it suited his convoluted political purposes. They even abandoned Qumran for a time, but reopened their community there during Jesus' childhood.

In 1894 an archaeologist, F. J. Bliss traced the line of the Hasmonean wall in Herod's time, and discovered what he identified as this gate. The Dominican Bagil Pixner re-excavated it a few years ago and found it to be only nine standard Roman feet wide, which suggests a semi-private entrance rather than a major public gate. Nearby, and just 'inside' he discovered remains of cisterns and mikvaot (baptisteries) which are certainly reminiscent of the Essene pre-occupation with repeated baptisms.

What does this mean to our quest for the Early Church? It offers fascinating possibilities. When Jesus sent two disciples to prepare the Passover, he told them to 'enter the city' (via a gateway; how else?) and look immediately for 'a man carrying a jar of water'. They were to exchange a verbal signal, and he would lead them to 'a large upper room all furnished' (Luke 22:7-12). A man carrying water suggests a signal, since that task normally fell to women. This is heightened by the fact that Essenes living in cities were obligated to chastity; there were no women to do the work !

Now one of the minor mysteries of the Gospel narratives involves the date of the Last Supper. Was it held on the evening of Passover (that is, during its first few hours, since the day began at sunset)? This is what Matthew, Mark and Luke clearly imply. But in that case how can John maintain that Passover was next day, and that the Jewish authorities had problems bringing Jesus to trial before Pilate? 'By now it was early morning, and to avoid ceremonial uncleanness the Jews did not enter the palace; they wanted to be able to eat the Passover' (John 18:28). There are several suggested solutions to this puzzle, but one of them is based on the realisation that the Supper itself happened in the Essene Quarter. For we know that the Essenes underlined their differences with the establishment by running their own liturgical calendar. They celebrated Passover the day before the others!

We can now see how Jesus could have celebrated Passover on the south-west Essene hill on *their* Passover day, and yet been crucified at the instigation of the Sadducees on *theirs*. This enables John to see symbolic significance in the fact that Jesus expired at the very time that the Passover lambs were being slain.

Shared Goods

There are other intriguing links between the Essenes and the Christians on the south-west hill. Immediately after Pentecost the disciples instituted a 'shared life' (koinonia) in which 'all the believers were together and had everything in common. Selling their possessions and goods, they gave to anyone as he had need' (Acts 2: 44-45). This sounds like an echo of the Essene custom.[11]

The 'Rule of the Community' found in Cave 1 at Qumran describes how new recruits passed through a phased membership procedure. First they made a novitiatory vow, accompanied by immersion in water. Then their property was provisionally surrendered to the Movement and held in trust, to be reclaimed if full membership was not pursued. They experienced the common life whilst continuing to work at their daily employment. Philo describes how 'Each member, when he has received the wages of their different occupations, gives it to one person who has been appointed as treasurer. He takes it and at once buys what is necessary... thus having each day a common life and a common table they are content'.[12]

Luke describes something similar in the earliest days, when the Upper Room was the main centre of the apostles' activity. Clearly the enthusiastic experiment did not last. There were logistical reasons why it could not. Essene communities were small (two hundred at most?), but converts were joining the church by the thousand. Chapter 4 of Acts shows the voluntary scheme still working ('they shared everything they had', verses 32-35). Then Joseph Barnabas sells *some* of his property for the common fund (verses 36, 37). But as numbers grew, different ways were found to express 'the fellowship', like a special collection to meet emergencies (Acts 11:27-30), and a weekly collection during worship, where people gave in proportion to their income (1 Cor. 16:1-4).

The rather perplexing tale of Ananias and Sapphira shows the scheme misfiring (Acts 5:1-11). But notice what the miserable couple had actually done. At some point rather like the second phase of Essene voluntary membership, they lied about the extent of their commitment. But Peter says, 'Didn't it belong to you before it was sold?', literally, 'when

it remained, did it not remain yours?' Does this describe the
situation in the initial trial period?

Peter adds: 'And after it was sold, wasn't the money at
your disposal?' Does that refer to a further stage, similar to
that of the Essenes, when the church actually held the money,
but only in trust? The offence of the couple was that 'you
have *lied* not to men but to God.' One of the Dead Sea Scrolls
uses similar language: 'If one of them has *lied* deliberately,
he shall be excluded from the Pure Meal of the Congregation.'

Here are several hints, then, that two religious communities centred in the same few acres of the city, had some practices in common. The Christian need not fear that this obser-
vation in some way diminishes the early disciples, as if they
should not have borrowed anything from their Jewish com-
patriots. As I have commented already (pp. 33-36), it is
hardly surprising that people addressing the same subjects
should come to some similar conclusions, especially when
they shared the same Hebrew Bible and the same prophetic
hopes!

Thus, the Essenes held that God was building a living
'temple' made up of those who trust God and obey him; a
familiar theme in Peter's and Stephen's preaching. The very
way in which James and Peter interpreted God's action in
Jesus and the church by invoking the prophets in a particular
way closely resembles at least one school of thought amongst
the Pharisees. Even the hints of how the church in Jerusalem
prayed in the temple and in small groups, and the way they
interpreted the psalms in their prayers are exactly what we
would expect to hear in Jerusalem at that very time.[13]

My story of the south-west hill has been long and
convoluted. Its tale of wandering tombs may not arouse
confidence in the integrity of holy sites! My enthusiasm in

THE SAVIOUR

putting the clues together may reveal more of my penchant for Sherlock Holmes and Father Brown than my acumen as an investigative historian. Not everyone is moved by the sight of archaeologists drawing large conclusions from small piles of stones. But I have to admit to profound emotion whenever I walk those streets and gardens once more, or even just look at my photographs back in Britain. For I too belong to that apostolic succession of faith. I too have 'called on the name of the Lord to be saved', as Peter urged. I too know something (and desire to know more) of the power of God's Spirit to change my life-style. I too treasure what it means to belong to a Koinonia-Fellowship that spans the centuries and crosses every cultural barrier. I too wish to be a living stone, built into a holy temple for the Lord.

And this is not a matter of myth and mysticism, of ideal and theory. In this city Jesus who was God incarnate lived and died and rose again, leaving an empty tomb behind, not just a hope of something after death. In this city new life was planted in the hearts of real men and women, not heroes in some fictional saga. Jerusalem was no fantasy Camelot, but a real city in which real people found a new dynamic and dimension of living in Jesus and his gospel. They learned, with many mistakes along the way, what it means to build a community of faith, truth and love.

References

1. *Biblical Archaeology Review*, May-June 1990, Vol. xvi, no. 3. I draw much of my material in this chapter from Bargil Pixner's article therein, 'Church of the Apostles found on Mount Zion', and from several chapters in *The Book of Acts in its First Century Setting*, vol. 4, *The Palestinian Setting*, edited by Richard Bauckham, Eerdmans-Paternoster, 1995.

2. James and the Jerusalem Church. Josephus the Jewish historian and Eusebius the 'father' of church history both give details of James, his leadership and his death. For a modern study of the neglected Jewish Church of the first four centuries, see *Nazarene Jewish Christianity* by Ray Pritz, Magnes Press, 1988. The Judaeo-Christians of the first four centuries have had little sympathy from the wider church. Because one group, the Ebionites (God's Poor) were adoptionist in their Christology, the whole movement is often unjustly assumed to have been heretical.

3. J. E. Dean, *Epiphanius' Treatise on the Weights and Measures, the Syriac Version*, Chicago, University Press, 1953, p. 30.

4. Egeria's *Travels to the Holy Land*, translation by J. Wilkinson. Aris & Philips, 1981, pp. 157-8.

5. Eusebius has slightly contradictory accounts of the flight to Pella, in his *Church History* and his *Proof of the Gospel*. In the tenth century the Patriarch of Alexandria gathered a lot of sources together to fill out the story. In the chaotic circumstances of AD 67-73, some confusion is hardly surprising.

6. David's burial, see 1 Kgs. 2:10, cf. 2 Sam. 5:6-9.

7. Dio Cassius (150-235), *Roman History* 69:14.

8. Baldi, *Enchiridian* no. 730. See Pixner's article, p. 28.

9. Pixner, 1990. pp. 31-34.

10. Josephus, Jewish War, para 145, p. 336

11. Baukham, chapter 11, 'The Palestinian cultural context of earliest Christian community of goods' by Brian J Capper, see especially pp. 337-340.

12. Philo, Hypothetica 11:10-11, see Bauckham, p. 353.

13. Bauckham, chapter 9, 'Jewish prayer literature and the Jerusalem Church in Acts' by Daniel K Falk.

14

Promise of New Life

Jerusalem still has its church today. The 'little house of God' on the south-west hill is a symbol of the enduring resilience of that organism of which Jesus said, 'The gates of hell shall not prevail against it' (Matt. 16:13-18).

He spoke those words in Banias, up in the Galilee Panhandle as it is known today. It is a beautiful region, in which two of the three sources of the river Jordan come gushing and spouting out of the hill-side, encouraging lush growth of trees, undergrowth and flowers. It is almost as if, at the source of the land's life, Jesus was asking his disciples about the source of their hopes. 'What do you think of me?'

Newly renamed Caesarea Philippi in honour of a king and an emperor, it stood at a vital T-junction of major routes connecting Mediterranean, Galilee, Lebanon and Syria. It was an appropriate place for Jesus to challenge the disciples as to their commitment to him and his mission. That mission would soon break across all social, religious, racial and cultural barriers, carrying the Word to every quarter, by these roads and others like them.

Panias (its original name) was a place of superstition and the occult, as well as military might and international trade. Pan represented the old gods (from his name we get 'panic', which meant superstitious fear). Where modern archaeologists are even now searching and rebuilding, niches in the rocky sides of Mount Hermon are still visible. They were once occupied by a pantheon (the word again) of the minute extra walk through the water tunnel is hard on back and legs, but well worth it! Biblical insights from Solomon to Book of Revelation.

Capernaum

This is a ruin, partly restored. Peter's House is almost certainly the HQ of Jesus and his disciples. Synagogue and street. Harbour. Nearby (walk or 5 minute coach) are Peter's Bay, Feeding of Five Thousand, Sermon on the Mount, and John 21 scene. All have very strong traditional and archaeological support. Try to linger, and have some private prayer.

Caesarea Philippi

Otherwise known as Banyas. Ruin at present being excavated and restored. Remarkable insights to 'I will build my church'. View of Mount Hermon, the most likely site for the Transfiguration.

Beth Shean

Associated with King Saul. Astonishing Roman amphitheatre now restored.

Caesarea Maritime

Ruins partly restored. Peter and Cornelius. Pilate's capital. Crusader city. Another remarkable Roman theatre. Sing a hymn in it!

Tel Aviv

Israel's chief city, and the first Jewish metropolis to be built in nineteen centuries. Visit the Museum of the Diaspora for remarkable insights to Jewish life worldwide. Adjoining Tel Aviv is the little biblical port of Joppa, associated with Solomon, Jonah and Peter. Sometimes a brief but rewarding visit can be paid on the homeward journey to the airport.

SCRIPTURE INDEX

SUBJECT INDEX